A Bibliography of Family
Placement Literature:
A guide to publications on
children, parents and carers

To Lynda with love

A Bibliography of Family Placement Literature:

A guide to publications on children, parents and carers

Martin Shaw

B ritish
A gencies
for **A** doption
and **F** ostering

Published by
British Agencies for Adoption & Fostering
(BAAF)
Skyline House
200 Union Street
London SE1 0LY

**British Library Cataloguing in Publication
Data**
Bibliography of Family Placement
Literature: Guide to Publications on Children,
Families and Carers. — 2Rev.ed
  I. Shaw, Martin
  016.3627330941

  ISBN 1-873868-14-6

Designed by Andrew Haig & Associates
Typeset, printed and bound by Russell Press
(TU) in Great Britain

Contents

Introduction

The first edition of this publication – entitled *Family Placement for Children in Care: A guide to the literature* – appeared in 1988. Six years and a substantial Children Act later, the need for a revised edition grows steadily more pressing, even though many people (not least its compiler) still seem to find the first edition a useful source of reference.

The Children Act 1989 added to the reader's problems in two ways. First, there was a predictable flood of books and articles from academics driven by a combination of intellectual curiosity and a requirement to publish or be damned. Less expected was an increased willingness on the part of UK practitioners to commit their ideas and experience to paper rather than leave the writing to their academic colleagues. US social work literature has long been enriched by writing which springs directly from practice. We must hope that UK practitioners are gaining a similar degree of confidence.

The second source of confusion for readers at this stage stems from the fact that most research-based literature still derives from work undertaken pre-Children Act. How relevant and tranferable are the findings of such studies now that the language and legal bases of child care social work have changed so drastically?

The first edition gave compiler and reader an opportunity to recollect, if not in tranquillity at least with some sense of perspective, the major writings of the previous twenty years. Over such a period, the task of selection is helped by time itself, sorting out the books and journal articles with more lasting value from those of limited or transient interest. A period of five or six years does not offer this useful service and the process of selecting in and selecting out is that much more dependent on the judgment, interest, prejudice or whim of the compiler. Apart from an unrepentant prejudice against all variations on the theme of 'Getting Our Act Together', I have tried to be fair.

This second edition is not just a supplement to the first but is intended to stand in its own right as a practical guide to 'child care' literature relevant to policy and practice post-Children Act 1989. For reasons of space, quite a number of items listed in the first edition have been omitted but it would have been absurd to exclude everything published before 1989. Some judicious pruning has been necessary in an effort to preserve the best of the old and build on to it the best of the new, and in order to achieve this aim several working (ie. flexible) principles have been employed:

1. to ensure that the 'classic' (even if in some ways dated) texts do not get lost in the flood of new material
2. to preserve other older material on topics which may not at present be top priority but which are nonetheless potentially important
3. to avoid duplications, such as articles which have since grown into books, or minor variants of the same material addressed to different audiences
4. to restrict coverage to material readily available through libraries with ready access to the Inter-Library Loan service and worth the expense of seeking it out. This rule has been relaxed occasionally for topics on which there is little 'mainstream' literature.

As before, a starring system has been used: new or general readers may find the double-starred (**) material most approachable as an introduction to the particular topic; single-starred (*) material is recommended to those seeking to be updated. The presence or absence of stars should not be taken as a judgment on the actual quality of the material, though judgments of this kind inevitably creep into some of the annotations.

Subject matter
The main subject matter of this publication is the family placement of children who are looked after by the local authority (within the terms of the Children Act 1989) and children placed for adoption. To put family placement in context, there is material also on the child care system generally, though residential and group care are not included; nor is the enormous literature on child abuse and neglect, except where it refers directly to family placement. References are largely restricted to social work literature, though again there are some references to related legal and medical sources.

WH Auden once remarked that a poem is never finished, only abandoned. At a more modest creative level, this is also true of a bibliography. This guide does not attempt to be fully comprehensive but seeks to offer selective coverage of material published up to the end of 1993.

Format

The numbered items are presented in sequence beginning with general material on the child care system (Chapter 1), and moving on to Family Support (Chapter 2), Looking After Children (Chapter 3) and Adoption (Chapter 4). Each section and many of the subsections are prefaced by a brief commentary which, without embarking upon a review of the literature, is intended to set the references in context. In both commentary and notes, those writers whose work is included in this publication are shown in block capitals. Following normal bibliographical practice, articles are shown in roman and books in italic type.

Acknowledgements

I am indebted to a number of colleagues at the University of Leicester and elsewhere who have made this publication possible: Stephen Rawlinson and his colleagues in the University Library for their help, not least a crash course in library computer studies; library staff in the National Children's Bureau, for similar friendly service; Shaila Shah at BAAF, for her expert and sympathetic guidance throughout this project; and Jane Aldgate, our recently appointed Professor of Social Work, for her practical help and moral support during a period when she had quite enough to occupy her time. Most of all, I have to thank my wife Lynda Randall, not – as with many writers – "for typing innumerable drafts" but for understanding and not attempting to treat my compulsive cataloguing.

For all this advice, guidance and assistance, readers will doubtless find errors, omissions and misjudgments, for which I take full responsibility.

Martin Shaw
University of Leicester
School of Social Work

May 1994

1 Children, parents and the Children Act

No one can complain of a lack of official or unofficial guidance to the Children Act: the problem for beginners and experts alike, given the wealth of published material, is to find a way through the guidance. The obvious starting point is the Children Act itself, with the proviso that it is generally more worthwhile to invest in an annotated version (eg BAINHAM 011, MASSON & MORRIS 014) rather than in its pure HMSO form. The Masson & Morris is particularly useful in that it incorporates relevant material from Guidance and Regulations within one volume.

Two Department of Health publications – 002, 003 – offer authoritative accounts of the Act's philosophy and intentions. For managers and practitioners, the various volumes of Guidance and Regulations are essential reading: each contains valuable material sadly obscured by over-elaboration and repetition – perhaps *Reader's Digest* should have been commissioned to produce the final version.

Apart from its own materials, the Department of Health commissioned several organisations to produce training material prior to the implementation of the Act. Several of these are still available [015–019] and are useful for inducting new staff.

Critical reflections on the Act are to be found in EEKELAAR & DINGWALL 025, FREEMAN 026 and PARTON 032.

Law and legal issues

001   *Children Act 1989 – Guidance and Regulations (published by HMSO):
       vol 1 *Court orders* ISBN 0 11 321371 9
       vol 2 *Family support, day care and educational provision for young children* ISBN 0 11 321372 7
       vol 3 *Family placements* ISBN 0 11 321375 1
       vol 4 *Residential care* ISBN 0 11 321430 8

vol 5 *Independent schools* ISBN 0 11 321373 5
vol 6 *Children with disabilities* ISBN 0 11 321452 9
vol 7 *Guardians ad litem* ISBN 0 11 321471 5
vol 8 *Private fostering* 0 11 321473 1
vol 9 *Adoption issues* ISBN 0 11 321474 X
vol 10 *Index* ISBN 0 11 321474 X

Department of Health publications on the Children Act (HMSO)

002 ***An introduction to the Children Act 1989* (1990) 96pp ISBN 0 11 321254 2

003 ***The care of children: principles and practice in Regulations and Guidance* (1990) 24pp ISBN 0 11 321289 5

004 *Children Act 1989: the welfare of children in boarding schools: practice guidance* (1991) 58pp ISBN 0 11 321477 4

005 *Children Act Report 1992* Cmd 2144 110pp ISBN 0 10 121442 1

006 *Manual of practice guidance for guardians ad litem and reporting officers* (1992) 176pp ISBN 0 11 321495 2

007 **Patterns and outcomes in child placement – messages from current research and their implications* (1991) 168pp + inserts ISBN 0 11 321357 3

008 *Protecting children: a handbook for social workers* (1988) 96pp ISBN 0 11 321159 7

009 *Working together under the Children Act: a guide to arrangements for inter-agency co-operation for the protection of children from abuse* (1991) 135pp ISBN 0 11 321472 3

010 WELSH OFFICE SOCIAL SERVICES INSPECTORATE (1990) *Children Act 1989: crossover points between local authorities and other agencies or organisations* Welsh Office – Social Services Inspectorate, Wales 17pp

Legal commentaries on the Children Act

011 *BAINHAM A (1991) *Children – the new law: the Children Act 1989* Family Law (Jordan & Sons) 388pp ISBN 0 85308 115 8
Commentary and discussion of issues as well as full text of the Act.

012 **CULLEN D (1992) *Child care law: England and Wales* 3rd edition BAAF 44pp ISBN 1 873868 06 5

2

013 MacCLEOD SM & GILTINAN D (1992) *Child care law: Scotland* 3rd edition BAAF 40pp ISBN 1 873868 01 4
Useful guides for quick reference.

014 *MASSON J & MORRIS M (1992) *The Children Act manual* Sweet & Maxwell 502pp ISBN 0 421 46980 3
Text of the Children Act 1989 as amended, plus Court Rules and Additional Statutory Instruments, with comprehensive annotations.

Children Act training materials sponsored by Department of Health

015 ADCOCK M, WHITE R & HOLLOWS A (1991) *Child protection: a training and practice resource pack for work under the Children Act 1989* National Children's Bureau

016 FAMILY RIGHTS GROUP (1991) *The Children Act 1989: working in partnership with families* A five-day training programme for social workers and their managers, and allied professionals HMSO

017 OPEN UNIVERSITY *The Children Act 1989: putting it into practice* Open University P558.

018 SHAW M, MASSON J & BROCKLESBY E (1990) *Children in need and their families: a new approach – a guide to Part III of the Children Act 1989 for local authority councillors* University of Leicester: School of Social Work 56pp ISBN 0 9511996 1 7

019 SHAW M, MASSON J & BROCKLESBY E (1991) *Children in need and their families: a new approach – a manual for managers on Part III of the Children Act 1989* University of Leicester: School of Social Work 211pp plus appendix

Social work practice and the Children Act

020 **ALLEN N (1992) *Making sense of the Children Act: a guide for the social and welfare services* 2nd edn Longman 232pp ISBN 0 582 09827 0
Clear commentary, though full text of the Act itself not included.

021 BAAF *The Children Act 1989: implications for medical advisers* BAAF Practice Note 28

022 BAAF *The Children Act 1989: transitional arrangements* BAAF Practice Note 25

023 BRANDON M (1992) 'Anticipating the impact of the Children Act on

social work practice in child care' *Adoption & Fostering* 16, 2, 22-29
Small-scale study to test social workers' preparedness for the 1989 Act.

024   *BRAYE S & PRESTON-SHOOT M (1992) *Practising social work law*
BASW/Macmillan 210pp ISBN 0 333 56637 8
Sets social work law in the context of values, practice dilemmas and
decision-making issues, with plentiful case illustrations. Primarily intended
for students but more experienced child care workers will also find its
approach illuminating and informative.

025   *EEKELAAR J & DINGWALL R (1990) *The reform of child care law:
a practical guide to the Children Act 1989* Routledge 153pp
ISBN 0 415 01736 X
Introduction setting the Act in its historical and legal context.

026   *FREEMAN MDA (1992) *Children, their families and the law – working
with the Children Act* Macmillan 260pp ISBN 0 333 54591 5
Introduction to the Act, taking account also of Guidance and Regulations
and practice issues for social workers.

027   FREEMAN M (1993) 'Removing rights from adolescents' *Adoption &
Fostering* 17, 1, 14-21
Examines the complexities of the law on consent.

028   FROST N (1992) 'Implementing the Children Act 1989 in a hostile climate'
in Carter P, Jeffs T & Smith MK (eds) *Changing social work and welfare*
Open University Press ISBN 0 335 15756 4
Critical look at the Act from the viewpoint of local authorities seeking to
implement it in the real world.

029   KING M & TROWELL J (1992) *Children's welfare and the law: the limits
of legal intervention* Sage 150pp ISBN 0 8039 87315
Using case illustrations, the authors argue that many children are damaged
rather than helped by the legal process.

030   MALLINSON I (1992) *The Children Act – a social care guide* Whiting
& Birch 205pp ISBN 187117189
Introduction to the Act, Regulations and Guidance, text of the legislation
not included.

031   NATIONAL CHILDREN'S BUREAU (1992) *The Children Act 1989 and
disability* NCB Highlight no 109
One of the NCB's series of useful briefing notes. It incidentally highlights
the sadly limited amount of literature so far on disability in relation to the

Children Act. See also Chapter 2 on Family Support for other relevant material.

032   PARTON N (1991) *Governing the family: child care, child protection and the State* Macmillan 251pp ISBN 0 335 54122 7
Critical analysis of the Children Act in its social and political context.

033   RYBURN M (1991) 'The Children Act – power and empowerment' *Adoption & Fostering* 15, 3, 10-13
Paper looking ahead to the Children Act, ending with some questions for social workers to ask themselves with a view to empowering children and families.

034   SHAW M (1993) 'The Children Act 1989: one year on in Leicestershire' *Adoption & Fostering* 17, 2, 41-44
Report on stock-taking staff seminars in one local authority.

035   THOBURN J (1991) 'The Children Act 1989: balancing child welfare with the concept of partnership' *Journal of Social Welfare and Family Law* 331-344
Discussion paper focusing on children for whom long-term care away from the family home is needed.

Research, policy and practice

Not all the items noted in this section relate directly to the Children Act – some indeed predate it – but they continue to have relevance nonetheless. The collections of short papers edited by KAHAN 050 and MORGAN & RIGHTON 056 form an excellent introduction and HARDING's [045] analysis of four value perspectives in child care provides a helpful framework for understanding legislation, policy and practice.

036   BRENNAN CM (1990) *Directory of child rights and welfare* Woodhead-Faulkner 323pp ISBN 0 85941 672 0
Substantial guide to organisations and publications, professional and popular, on a wide range of child care issues.

037   BRYER M (1988) *Planning in child care: a guide for team leaders and their teams* BAAF 164pp ISBN 0 903534 76 2
Workbook designed for first-line managers, examining the various stages in working with children and families. Particular attention is given to planning in relation to teenagers, now a substantial proportion of the care population.

038 CLIFFORD B & POWELL D (1988) 'Child care practice in the Gloucester area' University of Birmingham *Social Services Research* 1, 21-33
Research study analysing efforts to prevent admission to care, decision making, work with children in care, parent-child contact, and planning for long-term care or return home.

039 DEPARTMENT OF HEALTH (1991) *Child abuse: a study of inquiry reports 1980-1989* HMSO 117pp ISBN 0 11 321391 3

040 DEPARTMENT OF HEALTH AND SOCIAL SECURITY (1985) *Social work decisions in child care: recent research findings and their implications* HMSO 73pp ISBN 0 11 321046 9
Useful digest and discussion of various research studies which helped to shape the philosophy of the Children Act 1989.

041 DEPARTMENT OF HEALTH SOCIAL SERVICES INSPECTORATE (1990) *Developing services for young people with disabilities – report on the progress of six local authorities towards implementing Section 5 and 6 of the Disabled Persons Act 1986* SSI

042 FEIN E & MALUCCIO AN (1992) 'Permanency planning: another remedy in jeopardy?' *Social Service Review* 66, 3, 335-348
Reviews the course of the 'permanency movement', its achievements and unanticipated effects – particularly the failure to develop preventive and rehabilitative services.

043 FREEMAN I & MONTGOMERY S (eds) (1988) *Child care: monitoring practice* Jessica Kingsley 133pp ISBN 1 85302 005 0
Papers derived from Strathclyde child care research into reception into care, reviews, adoption of babies, short-stay fostering and child protection practice.

044 FROST N & STEIN M (1989) *The politics of child welfare: inequality, power and change* Harvester Wheatsheaf 179pp ISBN 0 7450 0613 2
Authors set out the political context of child abuse, juvenile crime, care of the under-fives and separated children, and argue that child welfare can only be understood as a political process reflecting divisions in society around class, gender, race and disability.

045 **HARDING LF (1991) *Perspectives in child care policy* Longmans 246pp ISBN 0 582 08345 1
Illuminating analysis of child care policy from four value perspectives – *laissez-faire*, state paternalism, defence of the birth family, and children's rights – influencing policy and day-to-day practice.

046   HOWING PT, KOHN S, GAUDIN JM, KURTZ PD & WODARSKI JS
       (1992) 'Current research issues in child welfare' *Social Work Research &
       Abstracts* 28, 5-12
       Issues and research relating to child welfare policy, child abuse, foster care
       and adoption.

047   HUDSON J & GALAWAY B (eds)(1989) *State as parent: international
       research perspectives on interventions with young persons* Martinus
       Nijhoff Netherlands Kluwer Academic 462pp ISBN 0 7923 0492 6
       Thirty-five papers from an international conference covering a wide range
       of disciplines and dealing with research into the organisation of state
       intervention; young people in conflict with the law; child abuse; and
       children in care.

048   HUNT J (1993) *Local authority wardships before the Children Act: the
       baby or the bathwater?* HMSO 92pp ISBN 0 11 321571 1
       Study by the Socio-Legal Centre for Family Studies at Bristol University.

049   JAMES G & WADCOCK D (1985) *Signpost: a guide for a person given
       the responsibility of setting up a complaints procedure for young people
       in care* National Children's Bureau 10pp

050   **KAHAN B (ed) 1989) *Child care research, policy and practice* Hodder
       & Stoughton/Open University 286pp ISBN 0 340 51331 4
       Like MORGAN & RIGHTON 056 a useful collection of papers introducing
       a range of child care topics.

051   KNAPP M, BAINES B & FENYO A (1988) 'Consistencies and
       inconsistencies in child care placements' *British Journal of Social Work,*
       18 Supplement, 107-130
       Discussion of a methodology for identifying consistencies and
       inconsistencies in placement patterns.

052   MAIDMAN F (ed) (1984) *Child welfare: a source book of knowledge and
       practice* NY: Child Welfare League of America 454pp ISBN 0 87868
       236 8
       Compendium of practice wisdom with chapters on an ecological approach,
       child protection, community work, child neglect and abuse, foster care,
       residential care, adoption, unmarried parents, and adolescents. Appendices
       on problem-solving approach and assessment frameworks.

053   MACLEOD A (1993) *Servicing social services: local authority legal
       representation in child care cases, 1990-1991* Department of Health/
       HMSO 42pp ISBN 0 11 321572 X
       Study by the Socio-Legal Centre for Family Studies at Bristol University.

054 MALUCCIO AN, FEIN E & OLMSTEAD KA (1986) *Permanency planning for children: concepts and methods* Tavistock 328pp ISBN 0 422 78850 3
Already the classic text on permanency, with theoretical analysis and detailed practice guidelines for work with parents and children. Maluccio and his colleagues have somewhat revised their thinking on permanency since this publication – see ALDGATE et al 347.

055 MINTY B & ASHCROFT C (1988) *Child care and adult crime* Manchester University Press 224pp ISBN 0 7190 2469 2
Research study whose authors claim that, at least from the point of view of their subsequent criminal records, 'some children from very inadequate homes would benefit from being placed long-term in substitute care.'

056 **MORGAN S & RIGHTON P (eds)(1989) *Child care: concerns and conflicts* Hodder & Stoughton/Open University 279pp ISBN 0 340 51330 6
Excellent introductory reader on wide range of child care topics.

057 OWENS DJ (1988) 'Marriage and family in contemporary Britain: some implications for social work policy' *Adoption & Fostering*, 12, 4, 44-48

058 PARKER RA (1987) *A forward look at research on the child in care* Bristol Papers in Applied Social Studies 2, University of Bristol 60pp ISBN 0 86292 298 4

059 PECORA PJ, WHITTAKER JK, MALUCCIO AN & PLOTNICK RD (1992) *The child welfare challenge: policy, practice and research* Aldine de Gruyter 526pp ISBN 0 202 36082 2
Written as a textbook on child welfare for US students, but its reviews of research literature are of interest also to UK readers.

060 ROBBINS D (1990) *Child care policy: putting it in writing – a review of English local authorities' child care policy statements* HMSO 60pp ISBN 0 11 321285 2

061 SCHAFFER HR (1990) *Making decisions about children: psychological questions and answers* Blackwell 260pp ISBN 0 631 17167 3
Research reviews and quick reference on many common questions around bonding, parenting, working mothers, day care, effects of divorce, etc.

062 SOCIAL SERVICES INSPECTORATE (1992) *Court orders study: a study of local decision making about public law court applications* Department of Health 93pp
Research in four local authorities over the first six months of 1992.

063 STEIN TJ & RZEPNICKI TL (1983) *Decision making at child welfare*

intake: a handbook for practitioners NY: Child Welfare League of America 130pp ISBN 0 87868 213 9
Authors advocate a decision-making approach and offer a systematic guide (with flow charts) to each stage in the intake process. Addressed to US agencies, but readily translateable to the UK scene. Note also sequel 064.

064 STEIN TJ & RZEPNICKI TL (1983) *Decision making in child welfare services: intake and planning* Mass: Kluwer-Nijhoff Publishing 171pp ISBN 0 89838 138 X

065 STONE W & WARREN C (1987/88) *Protection or prevention: a critical look at the voluntary child care sector* Child Care (National Council of Voluntary Child Care Organisations) 182pp
Sixteen papers from a series of national seminars, organised under four headings: family, law, community and race.

066 THOBURN J (1986) 'Quality control in child care' *British Journal of Social Work* 16, 543-556

067 THOMAS C with MURCH M & HUNT J (1993) *The duration of care proceedings: replication study* Department of Health/HMSO 90pp ISBN 321570 3
Study by the Socio-Legal Centre for Family Studies at Bristol University.

068 VEERMAN PE (1991) *The rights of the child and the changing image of childhood* Martinus Nijhoff Publishers, London Kluwer Academic 656pp ISBN 0 7923 1250 3
Using a 'systemic quality of life' model, the author undertakes an impressive scholarly analysis of the changing concept of childhood, drawing on material from the work of pioneers in children's rights and Declarations and Conventions around the world.

Religion, racial origin, culture and language
The specific references to religion, racial origin, culture and language in the Act have already generated a fair amount of literature, largely geared to encouraging policy makers and practitioners in their obligation to take account of these elements in children's lives. Other titles relating specifically to foster family care and adoption will be found in the relevant chapters. The titles by GAMBE et al 077 and MACDONALD 081 were produced with the Children Act in mind and contain useful introductory material.

069 AHMED S, CHEETHAM J & SMALL J (eds) (1986) *Social work with*

black children and their families Batsford/BAAF 207pp
ISBN 0 7134 4889 X
Papers on a range of issues including day care for the under-fives, black
children in care, transracial placement, black self-concept, work with
women and children, and intermediate treatment.

070   BAAF *The Children Act 1989: importance of culture, race, religion and
language* BAAF Practice Note 26

071   BANKS N (1992) 'Some considerations of "racial" identification and
self-esteem when working with mixed ethnicity children and their mothers
as social services clients' University of Birmingham *Social Services
Review* 3, 32-41
Some of the experiences of children of black/white parents may be different
from those of children with black/black parents. Author discusses possible
implications for work with children of dual heritage.

072   BARN R (1993) *Black children in the public care system* Batsford/ BAAF
160pp ISBN 0 7134 7136 0
The first large-scale UK study of black children in care, based on evidence
gathered from over 500 cases in an inner city social services department.

073   BLACK D (1990) 'What do children need from parents?' *Adoption &
Fostering* 14, 1, 43-51
Article critical of some aspects of same race placement policies as not being
sufficiently grounded in research evidence. See also HAMMOND 078.

074   BUTT J, GORBACH P & AHMAD B (1992) *Equally fair? A report on
social services departments' development, implementation and monitoring
of services for the black and minority ethnic community* EMSS Project,
National Institute for Social Work.

075   COOMBE V & LITTLE A (eds)(1986) *Race and social work: a guide to
training* Tavistock 233pp ISBN 0 422 79380 9
Amongst these useful short papers on a wide range of social work issues
are several specifically concerned with child care – racism and the
under-fives (Durrant), black children in residential care (Coombe), setting
up a community foster action group (Ahmed), and finding and working
with families of Caribbean origin (James).

076   DEPARTMENT OF HEALTH SOCIAL SERVICES INSPECTORATE
(1990) *Issues of race and culture in the family placement of children*
Circular C1(90)2

077   *GAMBE D, GOMES J, KAPUR V, RANGEL M & STUBBS P (1992)

10

Improving practice with children and families CCETSW Northern Curriculum Development Project, Leeds 102pp ISBN 1 85719 006 8
Training materials produced by a CCETSW working party, primarily for Diploma in Social Work programmes but useful also for social work teams. Includes many useful references.

078 HAMMOND C (1990) 'BAAF and the placement needs of children from minority ethnic groups' *Adoption & Fostering* 14, 1, 52-53
Response to BLACK 073.

079 JOHNSON MRD (1985) *Race and care: an indexed bibliography of material on multi-cultural welfare services* University of Warwick Centre for Research in Ethnic Relations 36pp ISBN 0 948303 55 7
Useful bibliography with introductory note but no annotations on individual items.

080 JOHNSON MRD (1991) 'Race, social work and child care' in P Carter, T Jeffs and M Smith (eds) *Social Work and Social Welfare Yearbook 3* Open University Press ISBN 0 335 09795 2

081 *MACDONALD S (1991) *All equal under the Act? a practical guide to the Children Act 1989 for social workers* National Institute for Social Work Race Equality Unit 137pp ISBN 1 873912 01 3
Handbook primarily intended to help social work teams examine their own policies and practices and bring them into line with the needs of their areas. Contains much interesting and stimulating material.

082 ROWE J (1990) 'Research, race and child care placements' *Adoption & Fostering* 14, 2, 6-8
Useful short article on making sense of research findings and avoiding some common fallacies in interpretation.

083 ROYS P (1984) 'Ethnic minorities and the child welfare system' *International Journal of Social Psychiatry* 30, 1/2, 102-118
Writer warns against over-concentration on transracial placement debate at the expense of wider questions about the relationship between black families and the child welfare system in the UK.

084 SMITH P (1990) 'Children – race and culture' in National Children's Bureau *Working with the Children Act 1989* NCB

085 WALKER FC (1981) 'Cultural and ethnic issues in working with black families in the child welfare system' in PA SINANOGLU & AN MALUCCIO 282.
Writer discusses the particular situation of black families and argues for

better understanding of cultural and ethnic issues, including the use of informal helping systems and alternative community structures providing intensive service to families.

Working with children – general

A number of useful training packs have appeared in recent years (BATTY & BAYLEY 089, BIGGS & ROBSON 091, OPEN UNIVERSITY 110,111,112) designed for use with social work teams or student groups. BAAF also usefully publishes its background papers separately – 090, 092 – a more convenient form for private study. FAHLBERG 101 and JEWETT 106 remain clear first recommendations for beginners and experienced workers alike.

086 ALDGATE J & SIMMONDS J (1988)(eds) *Direct work with children: a guide for social work practitioners* Batsford/BAAF 148pp
ISBN 0 7134 5594 2
Papers covering a range of topics including the assessment of children's needs, working with children experiencing separation and loss and those emotionally damaged; permanency planning; black child/white worker issues; and working with adolescents.

087 ARCHARD D (1993) *Children: rights and childhood* Routledge 200pp
ISBN 0 415 08252 8
Philosophical study of children's rights, challenging some current thinking about the role of the State and family in child-rearing.

088 BAAF (1989) *After abuse: papers on caring and planning for a child who has been sexually abused* BAAF 40pp ISBN 0 903534 82 7

089 BATTY D & BAYLEY N (1984) *In touch with children* training pack BAAF
Five-day course with materials for up to 20 participants.

090 **BATTY D (ed) (1986) *Working with children* BAAF 120pp
ISBN 0 903534 65 7
Practice papers drawn from 089.

091 BIGGS V & ROBSON J (1992) *Court skills* training pack BAAF
ISBN 1 873868 04 9
Two-day training course for social workers, managers, guardians ad litem, and health and education professionals, on preparing for and presenting cases in court.

092   BIGGS V & ROBSON J (eds)(1992) *Developing your court skills* BAAF
88pp ISBN 1 873868 05 7
Background papers drawn from 091.

093   BRAITHWAITE C (1987) 'Direct work with children by residential and
field workers' *Adoption & Fostering* 11, 4, 25-28, 10

094   *CATHOLIC CHILDREN'S SOCIETY (1983) *Finding out about me:
games for the preparation of children for family placement* Surrey: Catholic
Children's Society 22pp
Derived from practice experience in the Society's Homefinding Unit at
Gravesend.

095   CHILDREN'S LEGAL CENTRE (1990) 'Being a witness' *Childright*
no 63, 9-16
Material for use with young children in preparation for their court
appearance as witnesses.

096   CHILDREN'S LEGAL CENTRE (1991) 'At what age can I ...?' *Childright*
no 73, 11-14
Useful summary of the legal position of children and young people at
different ages.

097   CHILDREN'S SOCIETY & A VOICE FOR THE CHILD IN CARE (1988)
Perspectives: young people and the care system 3 papers: *Substitute care:
who provides the parenting?; In search of another way (young offenders);
It's my life* Children's Society with Voice for the Child in Care

098   CORRIGAN M & FLOUD C (1990) 'A framework for direct work with
children in care' *Adoption & Fostering* 14, 3, 28-32
Article based on authors' work in Westminster SSD.

099   **CROMPTON M (1990) *Attending to children: direct work in social and
health care* Edward Arnold 130pp ISBN 0 340 52741 2
An imaginative and simply written book addressed to child care workers
in a variety of settings, with plentiful use of examples.

100   DILLENBURGER K (1992/93) 'Communicating with children: the use
of art in social work' *Practice* 6, 1, 126-134
Paper discussing the application of art therapy without elaborate training
or resources.

101   **FAHLBERG V (1994) *A child's journey through placement* BAAF
392pp ISBN 1 873861 13 8
Contains the theoretical knowledge base and skills necessary for

understanding, working with, and planning for children and their families. Required reading for students and experienced practitioners alike. Updates and adds to FAHLBERG V (1988) *Fitting the pieces together: the complete Fahlberg collection* BAAF ISBN 0 903534 78 9

Incorporating *Child development; Attachment and separation; Helping children when they must move; The child in placement: common behavioural problems*

102   FITZGERALD J (1987) 'Young people in the care system' *Adoption & Fostering* 11, 4, 18-21
Short paper critical of various aspects of the care system's response to and provision for young people.

103   GILDERSLEEVE G (1988) 'Skills in working with adolescents' *Adoption & Fostering* 12, 1, 23-25

104   HOPKINS J (1990) 'A competence based approach to the care of children' *Adoption & Fostering* 14, 4, 18-22
Article seeking to identify practice competences to be derived from the Department of Health's *Principles and Practice* 003.

105   ISAACS S & HICKMAN S (1987) 'Communicating with children after a murder' *Adoption & Fostering* 11, 4, 32-34

106   **JEWETT CL (1984) *Helping children cope with separation and loss* Batsford/BAAF 146pp ISBN 0 7134 4707 9
Clear, practical down-to-earth guide for anyone concerned with children experiencing separation and loss.

107   MANN P (1984) *Children in care revisited* Batsford/BAAF 199pp ISBN 0 7134 0929 0

108   NAYPIC *Who Cares?* quarterly magazine published by NCB and Westminster Social Services Department with Department of Health support

109   NSPCC/CHILDLINE (1993) *The child witness pack – helping children to cope* NSPCC
Pack containing three booklets to help prepare parents, carers and children for court proceedings.

110   OPEN UNIVERSITY *Caring for children and young people* P653
Introductory training pack for those working with other people's children.

111   OPEN UNIVERSITY *Working with children and young people* K254
Degree level pack.

112   OPEN UNIVERSITY *Investigative interviewing with children* trainer's
       pack K501 Open University Department of Health & Social Welfare
       Training pack for specialist social workers and police officers, managers
       and supervisors involved in child protection work.

113   PAGE R & CLARK GA (1987) *Who cares? young people in care speak
       out* National Children's Bureau 63pp
       Influential report of NCB workshops for young people in care, which led
       to the setting up of Who Cares? groups and eventually to the founding of
       the National Association of Young People in Care (NAYPIC).

114   PEAKE A & ROUF K (1990) *Working with sexually abused children* 2nd
       edition Children's Society ISBN 0 907324 39 8
       Resource pack, including story books, colouring book, leaflets and practice
       papers, for professionals working with children.

115   ROBERTS J (1993) 'The importance of self-esteem to children and young
       people separated from their families' *Adoption & Fostering* 17, 2, 48-50
       Outline of some methods and techniques for direct work.

116   ROSE E (1988) 'Art therapy – a brief guide' *Adoption & Fostering* 12, 1,
       48-50

117   RYAN T & WALKER R (1993) *Life story work* BAAF 68pp
       ISBN 1 873868 10 3
       Practical guide, with examples, to making and using life story books.

118   STANDING CONFERENCE ON SEXUALLY ABUSED CHILDREN
       (1989) *Child sexual abuse: an annotated bibliography* SCOSAC
       150 key references.

119   WEBSTER J (1990) 'Parenting for children of schizophrenic mothers'
       Adoption & Fostering 14, 2, 37-43
       Review of literature and report on small-scale study.

120   WEBSTER J (1992) 'Split in two: experiences of the children of
       schizophrenic mothers' *British Journal of Social Work* 22, 3, 309-329
       Study of children and families of 28 schizophrenic women to assess effects
       of disruption and other problems encountered. Various coping styles
       identified.

121   WEST J (1990) 'Children "in limbo"' *Adoption & Fostering* 14, 2, 11-15.
       Article drawing on author's experience of using play in her work with
       children.

Working with parents – general

Work with parents receives less practical attention in the literature than does work with children, which makes the FAMILY RIGHTS GROUP publications particularly welcome (see also 016). Perhaps we may look forward to fuller coverage when the philosophy of partnership with parents fully takes hold. (Note also 282.)

122   ADCOCK M & WHITE R (eds)(1985) *Good-enough parenting: a framework for assessment* BAAF 115pp ISBN 0 903534 57 6
Collection of papers on some crucial topics in child care planning, including assessing parenting; standards of parenting and the law; parenting and parenting failure; good-enough and bad-enough parenting; predicting a family's response to treatment; also checklists on attachment and a developmental progress.

123   BENJAMIN M & IRVING HH (1989) 'Shared parenting: critical review of the research literature' *Family & Conciliation Courts Review* 27, 2, 21-35

124   BROWN H & BAILY P (1990) *Working with children and families: so you think you know what's normal?* training pack Pavilion Publishing ISBN 1 87 1080 56 8
Half-day training for up to 24 people in two groups on issues around parenting and family life.

125   COX AD, PUCKERING C, POUND A & MILLS M (1987) 'The impact of maternal depression on young children' *Journal of Child Psychology and Psychiatry* 28, 917-928

126   **FAMILY RIGHTS GROUP (1990) *Getting going: tips for starting and running a local support group for families with children in care, home from care or involved in child protection proceedings* FRG

127   ISAAC BC, MINTY B & MORRISON RM (1986) 'Children in care – the association with mental disorder in the parents' *British Journal of Social Work* 16, 325-339.
Study suggesting mental illness may be a factor in a significant proportion of parents whose children enter care.

128   MARSH P (1990) 'Changing practice in child care – the Children Act 1989' *Adoption & Fostering* 14, 4, 27-30

129   McGLOIN P & TURNBULL A (1988) 'Parents at child abuse reviews' *Social Services Research* 17, 4, 12-21.

130 NATIONAL CONSUMER COUNCIL AND NATIONAL INSTITUTE FOR SOCIAL WORK (1988) *Open to complaints: guidelines for social services complaints procedures* NISW

131 QUINTON D & RUTTER M (1988) *Parenting breakdown: the making and breaking of inter-generational links* ESRC/DHSS, Avebury Gower Publishing Co 270pp ISBN 0 566 05582 1
Comparative studies – retrospective and prospective – of children who have experienced care and those in the general population, with a particular focus on continuities and discontinuities in parenting.

2   Family support

Since the Children Act, 'family support' has in the UK taken on a specific meaning which derives from Part III s17 and refers to services provided by local authorities for children in need and their families. For those who regard Part III – rather than child protection – as the central pillar of the Children Act, encouragement and food for thought are to be found in the writings of FULLER 136-137, GIBBONS and colleagues 141-143, GARDNER 138-139, HARDIKER et al 144-145 and, most recently, TRISELIOTIS & MARSH 159. See also 018 for briefing on the family support provisions of the Children Act.

Day care has had a higher profile recently, thanks particularly to the work of the NATIONAL CHILDREN'S BUREAU 169-171 and MELHUISH & MOSS and others at the Thomas Coram Research Institute 165-168.

Respite care has been a growth area over the last decade or more, eventually providing the model for 'accommodation' under the Children Act. ROBINSON and STALKER 179-182, separately and in combination, have built up a substantial body of work in this area, and ALDGATE and colleagues 175, 183-184 usefully demonstrate that as a mode of care it is not so simple as it appears at first glance.

Most of the literature on children looked after by local authorities is dealt with in Chapter 3 but the paper by BEBBINGTON & MILES 132 is essential preliminary reading, well conveying the nature and extent of the challenge to family support and other 'preventive' services.

General

132   **BEBBINGTON A & MILES J (1989) 'The background of children who enter local authority care' *British Journal of Social Work* 19, 349-368

133   COOLEY ML & UNGER DG (1991) 'The role of family support in

determining developmental outcomes in children of teen mothers' *Child Psychiatry & Human Development* 21, 217-234
Investigation of support factors and maternal characteristics. Models offered to explain process of child development in families of teenage mothers.

134 DEPARTMENT OF EDUCATION AND SCIENCE (1989) *A survey of the education of children living in temporary accommodation April-December 1989* HMI Report 178/90/NS

135 FRANKEL J (1988) 'Family-centered home-based services in child protection: a review of the research' *Social Service Review* 62, 1, 137-157
Review article challenging claims that the effectiveness and cost-efficiency of family-centred, home-based services are well established. Part of the problem is the lack of properly controlled studies.

136 FULLER R (1989) 'Problems and possibilities in studying preventive work' *Adoption & Fostering* 13, 1, 9-13

137 FULLER R (1993) *In search of prevention: evaluative studies in social work* Avebury 121pp ISBN 1 85628 349 6

138 GARDNER R (1990) 'Prevention of family breakdown: a development project at the National Children's Bureau' *Adoption & Fostering* 14, 4, 23-26
Discussion of three recent studies in the area of prevention.

139 GARDNER R (1991) *Supporting families – preventive social work in practice* National Children's Bureau 331pp ISBN 0 902 817 922
Report of a development project in two social services areas to find out more about how parents saw their own needs for support and what resources they found useful.

140 GARDNER R & MANBY M (1993) 'The Children Act and family support: a crisis of values' *Adoption & Fostering* 17, 3, 20-25
Authors examine issues raised in the implementation of Part III, including the priority given to 'risk' as against 'need', partnership and protection, and some consequences of the purchaser-provider split.

141 GIBBONS J (1991) 'Children in need and their families: outcomes of referral to social services' *British Journal of Social Work* 21, 217-227
Describes attempts to devise measures of effectiveness of services using indicators of family needs, services received and outcomes.

142 **GIBBONS J (ed) (1992) *The Children Act 1989 and family support: principles into practice* HMSO 187pp ISBN 0113215495

Papers on a range of initiatives in relation to family centres, carers, children with disabilities, partnership with parents, child protection and policy development.

143 GIBBONS J, THORPE S & WILKINSON P (1990) *Family support and prevention: studies in local areas – purposes and organisation of preventive work with families* HMSO 200pp ISBN 0 11 701493 1

144 HARDIKER P, EXTON K & BARKER M (1991) 'The social policy contexts of prevention in child care' *British Journal of Social Work* 21, 341-359

145 *HARDIKER P, EXTON K & BARKER M (1991) *Policies and practices in preventive child care* Avebury 188pp ISBN 1 85628 108 6
Illuminating exploration of the concept of prevention both theoretically and in relation to data gathered in two local authorities.

146 HEATON K & SAYER J (1992) *Community development and child welfare* Children's Society 47pp ISBN 0 902406 81 7
Paper advocating a community-oriented approach to children and families.

147 HOLMAN R (1988) *Putting families first: prevention and child care* Macmillan 250pp ISBN 0 333 43793 4

148 HUBERT J (1991) *Home bound: crisis in the care of young people with severe learning difficulties* London: King's Fund Centre 195pp ISBN 0 903060 87 6
Account of the experiences of twenty families.

149 JONES MA (1985) *A second chance for families: five years later: follow-up of a program to prevent foster care* NY: Child Welfare League of America 161pp ISBN 0 87868 229 5
Study of two groups of families randomly assigned for 'ordinary' or 'special' social work help, showing a tendency for many children to come into care after withdrawal of 'special' services, but for shorter periods than those in the 'ordinary' group.

150 McCROSKEY J, NISHIMOTO R & SUBRAMANIAM I (1991) 'Assessment in family support programs: initial reliability and validity testing of the Family Assessment Form' *Child Welfare* 70, 1, 19-33
Report of progress in developing a Family Assessment Form for use in 'in-home' services.

151 NELSON KE, LANDSMAN MJ & DEUTELBAUM W (1990) 'Three models of family-centered placement prevention services' *Child Welfare* 69, 1, 3-21

Authors identify three distinct models of service, set out principal similarities and differences, and lay the groundwork for further research.

152 RANDHAWA M (1985) 'Prevention and rehabilitation with black families' *Adoption & Fostering* 9, 3, 42-43
Brief review of special features of work with black families.

153 ROSENTHAL JA & GLASS GV (1990) 'Comparative impacts of alternatives to adolescent placement' *Journal of Social Service Research* 13, 3, 19-37
US comparative study of day treatment, family treatment and foster care programmes for adolescents.

154 SCHORR LB (1991) 'Children, families and the cycle of disadvantage' *Canadian Journal of Psychiatry* 36, 437-441
Author concludes that programmes for children in disadvantaged families can reduce rates of truancy, teenage pregnancy, serious delinquency and dependence on welfare services.

155 SEABERG JR (1988) 'Child well-being scales: a critique' *Social Work Research & Abstracts* 24, 3, 9-15
US Child Well-Being scales attempt to provide specific measures to assist in the decision whether a child should be placed in care or should remain at home. Author discusses the scales and urges caution in their use.

156 SHEPPARD M (1993) 'Maternal depression and child care: the significance for social work and social work research' *Adoption & Fostering* 17, 2, 10-16
Article suggesting that greater attention to depression in mothers might reduce the need for children to be looked after by local authorities.

157 TELLEEN S, HERZOG A & KILBANE TL (1989) 'Impact of a family support program on mothers' social support and parenting stress' *American Journal of Orthopsychiatry* 59, 410-419
Account of support programme with two elements – mothers' self-help discussion group and parent education group – intended to increase support and reduce stress.

158 TIZARD B (1986) *The care of young children: implications of recent research* Thomas Coram Research Unit 46pp ISBN 0 85473 249 7

159 **TRISELIOTIS J & MARSH P (ed) (1993) *Prevention and reunification* Batsford/BAAF 196pp ISBN 0 7134 7104 2
Collection of papers exploring a range of topics including partnership, family support (including respite care), the differing experiences of black

and white children and families, support groups, and children and parents in the care system.

160 UNGER DG & NELSON P (1991) 'Evaluating community-based parenting support programs: successes and lessons learned from empowering parents of adolescents' *Journal of Applied Social Sciences* 15, 125-152

161 WHITTAKER JK, KINNEY J, TRACY EM & BOOTH C (eds)(1990) *Reaching high risk families: intensive family preservation services* Aldine de Gruyter 206pp ISBN 0 202 36058 X
Ten papers by US writers including Barth, Maluccio and Pecora, reviewing aspects of the Homebuilders model of family support, first developed in Washington State and employing an intensive approach to family services.

Day care

162 GOLDSCHMIED E (1993) *People under three: young children in day care* Routledge 240pp ISBN 0 415 05976 3
Practical guidance for managers and practitioners concerned with day care and family centres.

163 LINDON J & LINDON L (1988) 'Achieving quality in day care for young children' *Children & Society* 2, 2, 102-116
Argues that day care service must tackle definition of quality and move to a positive evaluation of what quality can mean.

164 McGURK H, CAPLAN M, HENNESSY E & MOSS P (1993) 'Controversy, theory and social context in contemporary day care research' *Journal of Child Psychology & Psychiatry & Allied Disciplines* 34, 1, 3-23
Review article critical of research and policy based on narrow assumptions about the needs of children.

165 MELHUISH E & MOSS P (eds)(1991) *Day care for young children: international perspectives* Routledge 225pp ISBN 0 415 01746 7

166 MOSS P & MELHUISH E (1991) *Current issues in day care for young children* HMSO 140pp ISBN 0 11 321337 9
Discussion of findings on day care research from UK, Sweden and the USA.

167 MOSS P (1986) *Child care in the early months: how child care arrangements are made for babies* Thomas Coram Research Unit, University of London Institute of Education 59pp ISBN 0 85473 255 1
Research study.

168 MOSS P (1987) *A review of childminding research* Thomas Coram

Research Unit, University of London Institute of Education 48pp
ISBN 0 843 274 8

169   NATIONAL CHILDREN'S BUREAU (1991) *Young children in group
day care – guidelines for good practice* National Children's Bureau 87pp
ISBN 0 902 817 72 8
Code of practice produced by an NCB working party.

170   NATIONAL CHILDREN'S BUREAU (1993) *Day care for children under
three* NCB Highlight no 116

171   NATIONAL CHILDREN'S BUREAU (1993) *Family-based day care* NCB
Highlight no 110

Family centres

172   CANNAN C (1992) *Changing families, changing welfare: family centres
and the welfare state* Herts: Harvester Wheatsheaf 180pp ISBN 0 7450
1183 7
Review of the history and function of family centres and the values
underpinning their creation.

173   FELLS JR & De GRUCHY S (1991) 'Exploring the "need" for family
centres: the perceptions of social workers and their importance for
planning' *British Journal of Social Work* 21, 173-184
Small study examining what social workers meant when they said that a
family needed a family centre, and the subsequent history of the
department's contact with those families in the absence of this resource.

174   HOLMAN B (1987) 'Family centres' *Children & Society* 1, 2, 157-173
Three models of family centres, how they serve different kinds of
consumers and fit best into statutory and voluntary sectors.

Respite care and refuges

175   ALDGATE J, PRATT R & DUGGAN M (1989) 'Using care away from
home to prevent family breakdown' *Adoption & Fostering* 13, 2, 32-37

176   NATIONAL CHILDREN'S BUREAU (1992) *Respite care* NCB Highlight
no 108

177   NEWMAN C (1989) *Young runaways: findings from Britain's first safe
house* Children's Society 157pp ISBN0 907324 51 7
Account of the work of the Central London Teenage Project, with feedback
from users, parents and social workers, and discussion of wider matters
arising.

178   PARKINSON K (1991) *Respite care for children with disabilities in North-East Essex* Essex County Council
Questionnaire study of parents' use of respite services.

179   ROBINSON C & STALKER K (1989) *Time for a break: respite care – a study of providers, carers and patterns of use* Bristol University: Norah Fry Research Centre

180   ROBINSON C & STALKER K (1993) 'Patterns of provision in respite care and the Children Act' *British Journal of Social Work* 23, 1, 45-63
Report of a three-year study funded by the Department of Health into respite care services for children with disabilities.

181   ROBINSON C (1991) *Home and away: respite care in the community* Birmingham: Venture Press 111pp
Practical guide to establishing and running a family-based respite care service.

182   STALKER K (1990) *Share the care: an evaluation of a family-based respite care service* Jessica Kingsley Publishers 160pp ISBN 1 85302 038 9

183   WEBB SA (1990) 'Preventing reception into care: a literature review of respite care' *Adoption & Fostering* 14, 2, 21-27

184   WEBB SA & ALDGATE J (1991) 'Using respite care to prevent long-term family breakdown' *Adoption & Fostering* 15, 1, 6-13
Report of a study testing the feasibility of using respite care in a local authority social services department.

3   Looking after children

The Children Act 1989 has dramatically altered language and thinking around what used to be called 'children in care'. The umbrella term is now children 'looked after' (ie. by the local authority). These children fall into two subgroups – those 'in care' following a court order and those who are 'accommodated' by agreement with the parents.

The use of the term 'in care' to cover both subgroups will of course be found in pre-1989 UK publications and in North American literature still. Somewhat illogically, the terms 'aftercare' and 'leaving care' continue to be used across the board, simply because life is too short to keep referring to after-being-looked-after or leaving-being-looked-after by the local authority.

The changes introduced by the Children Act are more than matters of terminology. 'Accommodation' of children by the local authority is to be seen as part of a programme of family support rather than as a sign of failure to keep child and family together. The model is that of respite care, intended as a non-stigmatising and relatively informal partnership between parents, carers and local authority. Literature on 'accommodated' children might logically be assigned to the Family Support chapter but it is felt that for the moment this would lead to confusion, given that most of the material in the present chapter predates the 1989 Act. For convenience, literature on respite care will be found under Family Support 175-184, while material on other varieties of foster family care appears below.

Some North American writing on 'foster care' and 'foster homes' includes residential as well as family care. Placement with a family is referred to more specifically as 'foster family care'.

General

As introductions to the development of child care services generally before the Children Act 1989, PACKMAN 209 and HEYWOOD 200 (the latter obviously less up-to-date) remain unsurpassed. The 1980s were a fruitful period for research on children in and around the care system and the studies cited below (FISHER et al 194, MILLHAM et al 206, PACKMAN et al 210, ROWE et al 256, VERNON & FRUIN 224) continue to repay careful study. These and other studies are usefully summarised in 040. Of more recent studies, ROWE et al 214 is a major work, challenging many preconceptions about children in the care system.

185   ALDGATE J (ed) (1985) *Using written agreements with children and families* Family Rights Group 77pp ISBN 1 871515 01 7
Collection of papers by various writers including Celia Atherton, Anthony Maluccio and Jane Tunstill.

186   BATTY D & ROBSON J (1991) *Managing statutory reviews* training pack BAAF ISBN 1 873868 03 0
One-day training on the review process, with trainers' notes and participants' workbooks.

187   BATTY D & ROBSON J (1991) *Statutory reviews in practice* BAAF 68pp ISBN 1 873868 02 2
Papers derived from above training pack.

188   BENEDICT M & WHITE RB (1990) 'Factors associated with foster care length of stay' *Child Welfare* 70, 1, 45-58.
Maryland study which confirms previous research findings and adds as important factors the child's physical health and development and school performance, and parental inability or unwillingness to work constructively with agency.

189   BULLARD E & MALOS E with PARKER RA (1991) *Custodianship: caring for other people's children* HMSO 262pp ISBN 0 11 321348 4
Research study into a short-lived mode of care which may in retrospect be seen as having prepared the way for open adoption.

190   CLIFFE D & BERRIDGE D (1991) *Closing children's homes: an end to residential childcare?* National Children's Bureau 245pp ISBN 0 902 817 80 9
Study of Warwickshire's experiment in closing down residential establishments in favour of family placement, showing positive gains but cautioning others against wholesale switching to family placement without careful preparation.

191 CLINE T (1989) 'Making case conferences more effective: a checklist for monitoring and training' *Children & Society* 3, 2, 99-106
Observation checklist for participants for monitoring effectiveness. Proposes detailed examination of preparation, initiation of discussion, the decision process, participants' behaviour, and involvement of parents, guardians and children.

192 COLTON MJ (1988) *Dimensions of substitute child care: comparative study of foster and residential care practice* Avebury Publishing Company 289pp ISBN 0 566 05612 7
A detailed study which found, amongst other things, that foster care practices are the more child-oriented.

193 COLTON M, ALDGATE J & HEATH A (1990-91) 'Behavioural problems among children in and out of care' *Social Work and Social Sciences Review* 2, 3, 177-191
Comparative study showing high levels of behavioural problems among foster children, but even greater levels among children in families receiving preventive help from social services.

194 *FISHER M, MARSH P, PHILLIPS D & SAINSBURY E (1986) *In and out of care: the experiences of children, parents and social workers* Batsford/BAAF 154pp ISBN 0 7134 5340 0
Sheffield study involving interviews with social workers, parents and children, followed up over 12 months. Study highlights differences in the various parties' perceptions at each stage of the care process.

195 *FITZGERALD J (1990) *Understanding disruption* 2nd edition BAAF 48pp ISBN 0 903534 92 4
Revised and updated handbook with guidelines and useful checklists for dealing with unplanned endings in adoption and foster family placements.

196 FULLER R (1985) *Issues in the assessment of children in care* National Children's Bureau 45pp

197 GARDNER R (1987) *Who says? choice and control in care* National Children's Bureau 106pp ISBN 902817 36 1
Interviews with 50 young people and their carers.

198 GRIMSHAW R & SUMNERS M (1991) *What's happening to child care assessment? an exploratory study of new approaches* National Children's Bureau 268pp 0 902 817 78 7

199 HARRIS R & TIMMS N (1993) *Secure accommodation in child care: 'between hospital and prison or thereabouts?'* Routledge 208pp

ISBN 0 415 06282 9
Major study on the use of secure accommodation and how it is viewed by courts, social workers and young people themselves.

200 **HEYWOOD, JS (1978) *Children in care* 3rd edition Routledge & Kegan Paul 284pp ISBN 0 7100 8733 0
Historical study of the development of attitudes to and services for children 'deprived of a normal home life'.

201 HILL M (1992) 'Fostering and adoption in Canada: are there lessons for Britain?' *Adoption & Fostering* 16, 4, 39-44
Reflections after a visit to Canadian child care agencies.

202 HOGGAN P (1991) 'The role of children in permanency planning' *Adoption & Fostering* 15, 4, 31-34
Author argues that the protectionist stance in Scottish society restricts efforts to involve children in planning.

203 HOLMAN B (ed) (1988) *Planning for children* Family Rights Group 133pp ISBN 1 871515 02 5
Fourteen papers from FRG seminars on a wide range of topics around the placement and rehabilitation of children.

204 KATZ L & ROBINSON C (1991) 'Foster care drift: a risk-assessment matrix' *Child Welfare* 70, 3, 347-358
Authors present a matrix linking problems with specific intervention strategies which they have found helpful in identifying and assisting children and families most at risk of drift.

205 LINDSEY D (1991) 'Factors affecting the foster care placement decision: an analysis of national survey data' *American Journal of Orthopsychiatry* 61, 272-281
US research into reasons why some children come into care while others with similar problems do not. Concludes that for children in all age groups parents' income is the best predictor.

206 *MILLHAM S, BULLOCK R, HOSIE K & HAAK M (1986) *Lost in care: the problems of maintaining links between children in care and their families* Gower 258pp ISBN 0 566 00998 6
Study of the links between parents and their children in care, the nature of these links and problems in maintaining them.

207 MILLS K (1992) 'Services for adolescents in South Glamorgan' University of Birmingham *Social Services Review* 3, 1-31
Study and evaluation of a wide range of services, including family placement.

208 NUNNO M & RINDFLEISH N (1992) 'The abuse of children in out-of-home care' *Children & Society* 5, 4, 295-305
US study noting that children removed from home in 'child protection' proceedings are referred following further abuse two or three times as often as children living with their own families. Implications are discussed.

209 **PACKMAN J (1981) *The child's generation: child care policy in Britain* 2nd edition Basil Blackwell & Martin Robertson 202pp. ISBN 0 631 12664 3
Excellent introduction to the historical development of the child care service from World War II till around 1980.

210 *PACKMAN J, RANDALL J & JACQUES N (1986) *Who needs care? social work decisions about children* Basil Blackwell 221pp ISBN 0 631 14374 2
Study of children in two local authorities – analysed in terms of 'volunteers', 'victims' and villains' – which revealed interesting differences in the agencies' policies and practices. Use of admission to care only as a last resort found to be inappropriate, resulting in ill-planned, emergency admissions, and experienced as unhelpful by the families concerned.

211 *PARKER R, WARD H, JACKSON S & ALDGATE J (eds)(1991) *Looking after children – assessing outcomes in child care* HMSO 204pp ISBN 0 11 321459 6
Discussion of theoretical issues relating to outcome measurement in child care. Supplementary materials (below) published separately:
Looking after children – assessment and action records HMSO ISBN 0 11 321561/6 Separate records for children aged under 1 year; 1-2 years; 3-4 years; 5-9 years; 10-15 years; and over 16 years.
Looking after children – guidelines for users of the assessment and action records HMSO 28pp ISBN 0 11 321457 X

212 ROSE J (1987) *For the sake of the children: inside Dr Barnardo's – 120 years of caring for children* Hodder & Stoughton 335pp ISBN 0 340 37319 9
Absorbing, sympathetic but not uncritical history of Barnardo's.

213 ROWE J & LAMBERT L (1973) *Children who wait: a study of children needing substitute families* Association of British Adoption Agencies 195pp
The classic study which introduced UK social workers to the idea of 'drift' and the need for a radical approach to placement planning.

214　*ROWE J, HUNDLEBY M & GARNETT L (1989) *Child care now: a survey of placement patterns* BAAF 128pp ISBN 0 903534 85 1
Research study in six local authorities of all placements over a two-year period, challenging much received wisdom about children's care careers.

215　ROWE J, HUNDLEBY M & GARNETT L (1989) *Child care placements: patterns and outcomes* BAAF 316pp
As 214 plus questionnaires and full statistical analysis.

216　SEABERG JR (1988) 'Placement in permanency planning: own home versus foster care' *Social Work Research & Abstracts* 24, 4, 4-7
US study in which the writer analyses factors which appear to distinguish children who enter care from those remaining at home.

217　SELTZER MM & BLOKSBERG LM (1987) 'Permanency planning and its effects on foster children: a review of the literature' *Social Work* 32, 1, 65-68
Review of US research indicated higher rate of adoption achieved in agencies where permanency planning is accepted than where it was not; adoptions tended to be stable, a substantial minority of rehabilitations were not – rate of disruption from rehabilitation no lower since introduction of permanency planning than before.

218　STEINHAUER PD (1991) *The least detrimental alternative: a systematic guide to case planning and decision making for children in care* University of Toronto 426pp ISBN 0 8020 6836 7
Contains sections on the history of adoption and foster care, attachment, parenting capacity, placement, shared care, contact, the foster care system, sexual abuse within the fostering system, adoption, and the preventive use of foster care – covering a great deal, if somewhat sketchily.

219　**THOBURN J (1988) *Child placement: principles and practice* Wildwood House: Community Care Practice Handbook 123pp ISBN 0 7045 0583 5
Guide for practitioners on planning for and with children. Predates the 1989 Act but the principles expressed are very much in the spirit of the Act.

220　THOBURN J, MURDOCH A & O'BRIEN A (1987) *Permanence in child care* Blackwell 224pp ISBN 0 631 15097 8
Research study into the Children's Society project, *The Child Wants a Home*.

221　THORPE D (1988) 'Career patterns in child care – implications for service' *British Journal of Social Work* 18, 2, 137-153
Reports a research study of care careers of 231 children, and outlines

planning strategies for children who remain in care beyond six weeks and who would benefit by being restored to natural parents.

222 TRISELIOTIS J (1991) 'Permanency planning: perceptions of permanence' *Adoption & Fostering* 15, 4, 6-15
Discussion of the achievements of permanency planning and some problems arising.

223 TRISELIOTIS J (ed) (1980) *New developments in foster care and adoption* Routledge & Kegan Paul 243pp ISBN 0 7100 0461 3
Well, hardly new now – time for a second edition? – but still a useful collection of papers as an introduction to the area.

224 *VERNON J & FRUIN D (1986) *In care: a study of social work decision making* National Children's Bureau 157pp
Research study which found worrying levels of non-decision making in such key areas as parent–child contact in care, discharge from care, reviews and planning for children in care.

Education and health issues

After years of relative neglect, it is encouraging to see the education and – to a lesser extent – health care of children looked after by local authorities beginning to receive attention in the literature.

225 ALDGATE J (1990) 'Foster children at school: success or failure?' *Adoption & Fostering* 14, 4, 38-49
Review of research and account of a recent study undertaken at Oxford.

226 ALDGATE J, COLTON M, GHATE D & HEATH A (1992) 'Educational attainment and stability in long-term foster care' *Children & Society* 6, 2, 91-103
Study of reading attainment in 8-14 year olds in long-term care highlights the importance of stability rather than type of placement. No link discovered between attainment and contact with birth parents.

227 ALDGATE J, HEATH A, COLTON M & SIMM M (1993) 'Social work and the education of children in foster care' *Adoption & Fostering* 17, 3, 25-34
Report of a recent study with authors' recommendation that much more attention should be paid to the educational progress of children looked after by local authorities.

228 FLETCHER-CAMPBELL F (1990) 'In care? in school?' *Children & Society* 4, 4, 365-373

Draws upon NFER/ESRC-funded research reviewing the arrangements for the education of children in care. Explores issues and recommends research and new policies and practices.

229   FLETCHER-CAMPBELL F & HALL C (1991) *Changing schools? Changing people?* National Foundation for Educational Research 184pp ISBN 0 7005 12853
Series of studies of social services departments' policies and practices regarding the education of children in care, with predictably depressing results and recommendations for change.

230   HEATH A, COLTON M & ALDGATE J (1989) 'The educational progress of children in and out of care' *British Journal of Social Work* 19, 6, 447-460

231   HENDRIKS JH (1989) 'The health needs of young people in care' *Adoption & Fostering* 13, 1, 43-50

232   JACKSON S (1987) *The education of children in care* Bristol Papers in Applied Social Studies 1, University of Bristol 50pp ISBN 0 86292 297 6
Review of research, with recommendations for remedial action.

233   JACKSON S (1988) 'Education and children in care' *Adoption & Fostering* 12, 4, 6-10
Article derived from Bristol study 232.

234   NEWSOME M (1992) 'The impact of the past on the care and education of deprived children' *Children & Society* 6, 2, 151-162
Follows on from article in previous issue and shows how past attitudes are still prevalent in present-day policy and assumptions.

235   SIMMS M (1988) 'The health surveillance of children in care – are there serious problems?' *Adoption & Fostering* 12, 4, 20-23.

Foster family placement – general

ROWE 255 provides an excellent short introduction to issues in foster family care, though an update to take account of of the situation post-1989 Act would be most welcome. GEORGE 246 remains an essential text on the dilemmas and ambiguities of fostering, not least on the place of natural parents in the system.

236   ALDGATE J & HAWLEY D (1986) 'Helping foster families through disruption' *Adoption & Fostering* 10, 2, 44-49 & 58

237   ALDGATE J & HAWLEY D (1986) 'Preventing disruption in long-term

foster care' *Adoption & Fostering* 10, 3, 23-30
Two papers based on material gathered for the study noted below.

238 *ALDGATE J & HAWLEY D (1986) *Recollections of disruption: a study of foster care breakdowns* NFCA 76pp ISBN 0 946015 28 7
Oxfordshire study with findings on the effects of disruption on the foster family, preparation for placement, and the placement itself.

239 ASHFORD S & TIMMS N (1990) 'Values in social work: investigations of the practice of family placement' *British Journal of Social Work* 20, 1, 1-20
Study in several local authority and voluntary agencies of the values which family placement workers bring to their work.

240 ATKINSON C & HORNER A (1990) 'Private fostering – legislation and practice' *Adoption & Fostering* 14, 3, 17-22
Discusses the role of the African Family Advisory Service in what remains a little-explored area of family placement.

241 **BAAF (1992) *Foster care: some questions answered*
BAAF information leaflet for the general public.

242 *BERRIDGE D & CLEAVER H (1987) *Foster home breakdown* Basil Blackwell 234pp ISBN 0 631 15916 9
Extensive study to determine the incidence, causes and predictability of breakdown, involving interviews with social workers, foster parents, birth parents, children and school teachers.

243 **BULLOCK R (1990) 'The implications of recent child care research findings for foster care' *Adoption & Fostering* 14, 3, 43-45

244 FEIN E (1991) 'Issues in foster family care: where do we stand?' *American Journal of Orthopsychiatry* 61, 578-583
Survey of recent US research and some matters arising, including outcomes, crisis in fostering, and the vulnerable position of ethnic minority children.

245 FEIN E, MALUCCIO AN & KLUGER AN (1989) *No more partings* Washington DC: Child Welfare League of America 85pp. ISBN 0 87868 352 6
Connecticut study of long-term foster family placements, which concludes that this may be the placement of choice for some children, contrary to strict permanency thinking.

246 **GEORGE V (1970) *Foster care: theory and practice* Routledge & Kegan Paul 251pp ISBN 7100 6800 X

33

Classic study indicating the gap between foster theory and practice. Argues strongly the need to give much greater consideration to the place of birth parents and to reassess role of foster carers within the fostering system. Salutary to note that its messages remain relevant more than 20 years on.

247   HESS P & FOLARON G (1991) 'Ambivalences: a challenge to permanency for children' *Child Welfare* 70, 4, 403-424
       Study showing how parental uncertainty in planning for children may be reinforced by agency policy, working conditions and lack of resources.

248   *HOGHUGHI M & HIPGRAVE T (1985) *Towards a discipline of fostering* NFCA 32pp ISBN 0 946015 22 8
       Two papers arguing for and seeking to provide a theoretical basis for fostering practice.

249   HOLMAN R (1973) *Trading in children: a study of private fostering* Routledge & Kegan Paul 349pp ISBN 0 7100 7538 3
       Still the only major study of the Cinderellas of the foster care population.

250   *HOLMAN R (1975) 'The place of fostering in social work' *British Journal of Social Work* 9, 1, 3-29
       Classic paper arguing for an inclusive approach to foster family care by social workers and carers. Shorter version reprinted in Triseliotis 223.

251   HOREJSI CR (1979) *Foster family care: a handbook for social workers, allied professionals, and concerned citizens* Springfield, Illinois: Charles C Thomas 357pp ISBN 0 398 03898 8
       Handy guide to many aspects of foster family care, presented in (rather stilted) question-and-answer form.

252   KLINE D & OVERSTREET HMF (1972) *Foster care of children : nurture and treatment* Columbia University Press 316pp ISBN 0 231 08617 2
       Useful text on the theory and practice of foster family care.

253   NFCA (1990) *Put it in writing: agreeing a written placement plan in foster care* NFCA ISBN 0 94601 569 4
       Discusses the process of agreeing a plan and offers a possible model for agreements.

254   PARKER RA (1978) *Decision in child care: a study of prediction in fostering* Allen & Unwin 121pp
       Classic research study which sought to develop a prediction table for success and failure in foster family placement.

255   **ROWE J (1983) *Fostering in the eighties* BAAF 40pp

ISBN 0 903534 48 7
Discussion paper on issues current in foster care in the 1980s – and 90s.

256   ROWE J, CAIN H, HUNDLEBY M & KEANE A (1984) *Long-term foster care* Batsford/BAAF 255pp ISBN 0 7134 6014 4
Study of 200 foster children in five local authorities concluded that, with all its defects, there is a future for long-term fostering, particularly for older children who have strong bonds with their birth families. Contrary to the received wisdom of the time, placements with relatives were amongst the most successful of placements studied.

257   STONE J (1991) 'The tangled web of short-term foster care: unravelling the strands' *Adoption & Fostering* 15, 3, 4-9.
Author's account of her research into 183 placements of children with short-term foster carers over a twelve-month period, investigating the current role of short-term fostering and how it may be used to meet the needs of a range of different children.

258   **TRISELIOTIS J (1989) 'Foster care outcomes: a review of key research findings' *Adoption & Fostering*, 13, 3, 5-17
Review of research findings over a period of about 30 years.

259   TRISELIOTIS J (ed) (1988) *Groupwork in adoption and foster care* Batsford/BAAF 160pp ISBN 0 7134 5460 1
Papers on preparation and assessment of families, ethnic minority families, children, post-adoptive groups, specialist fostering, preparing adolescents.

Ethnic issues in foster family care

Although transracial placement remains a live issue in both literature and practice, it is encouraging to see the appearance of more material which offers positive guidance on recruiting and preparing 'same-race' carers (eg 260, 261, 267 and 268). See also 076 and 078 on 'same-race' policy, and 320 for some practice issues.

260   ALMAS T (1992) 'After recruitment: putting the preparation and training of Asian carers on the agenda' *Adoption & Fostering* 16, 3, 25-29
Article derived from project by New Families in Yorkshire – see also 267.

261   *CHARLES M, RASHID S & THOBURN J (1992) 'The placement of black children with permanent new families' *Adoption & Fostering* 16, 3, 13-19
Preliminary findings from a study of 241 black children and children of

35

other minority ethnic groups drawn from a large sample of children with special needs.

262 COMMISSION FOR RACIAL EQUALITY (1975) *Fostering black children* CRE 36pp
Discussion of issues, with recommendations.

263 *JENKINS S & DIAMOND B (1985) 'Ethnicity and foster care: census data as predictors of placement variables' *American Journal of Orthopsychiatry* 55, 2, 267-276
US study with some fascinating findings, eg. where black people are under-represented in an area, the chances of a black child being in care are twice as high as might be expected; but where black people are over-represented, black children are less likely to be in care.

264 KELLY C, CLARE S & STOBER J (1989) 'Black issues in child care – training for foster carers and adoptive parents *Adoption & Fostering* 13, 3, 29-33.

265 LOFTUS Y (1986) 'Black families and parental access' *Adoption & Fostering* 10, 4, 26-27
Writing from her experience in a London borough, the author notes that black carers are often more willing than white carers to maintain birth parents' involvement and to work towards reunification.

266 MULLENDER A (1988) 'Groupwork as the method of choice with black children in white foster homes' *Groupwork* 1, 2, 158-172
Whilst supporting the principle of 'same-race' placement, the writer is concerned to promote the well-being of children already placed transracially, and advocates groupwork as an effective means of enhancing self-esteem and sense of identity. A version of this paper also appears in 259.

267 *NEW FAMILIES IN YORKSHIRE (1991) *Fostering and adoption in Asian families: a guide for the preparation and training of Asian adoptive and foster families* New Families in Yorkshire, Barnardo's

268 *RACE EQUALITY UNIT (1993) *Black children and private fostering* National Institute for Social Work 78pp ISBN 1 873912 35 8
Report by a joint NISW/BAAF working party offering an historical context, the main issues and practical guidelines on policy, practice and procedures.

269 RHODES PJ (1992) *Racial matching in fostering: the challenge to social work practice* Avebury 318pp ISBN 1 85628 264 3

Discussion of issues with case studies derived from a research study in a London borough.

270 WOOLARD C (1991) 'Private fostering – a health concern' *Adoption & Fostering* 15, 3, 54-58
Issues for medical practitioners dealing with families in which Nigerian children are being privately fostered.

271 WRIGHT D (1992) 'Private fostering: public duty – private responsibility' *Adoption & Fostering* 16, 3, 30-34
Article derived from the experience of Save the Children's African Family Advisory Service.

Birth parents in foster family care

US writers still offer the most comprehensive material on involving and working with birth parents (eg 273 and 282; see also 054). ALDGATE 272 addresses more directly the UK scene post-Children Act.

272 *ALDGATE J (1991) 'Partnership with parents – fantasy or reality?' *Adoption & Fostering* 15, 2, 5-9
Discussion of practice issues in partnership with parents where children are accommodated or in care and away from home, advocating an ecological approach.

273 *BLUMENTHAL K & WEINBERG A (eds)(1984) *Establishing parent involvement in foster care agencies* NY: Child Welfare League of America 247pp ISBN 0 87868 214 7
After discussion of the importance of parental involvement, the authors examine the implications for agency staff at all levels. Useful appendices on agreements, reviews and policies geared to parental involvement.

274 JENKINS S & NORMAN E (1972) *Filial deprivation and foster care* NY: Columbia University Press 296pp ISBN 0 231 03575 6
Early study revealing the ambivalence and complexity of parental reactions to the loss of their children. Findings emphasise the need for urgent and intensive action if children are to be restored to their families.

275 *LEE JAB & NISIVOCCIA D (1989) *Walk a mile in my shoes – a book about biological parents for foster parents and social workers* NY: Child Welfare League of America 87pp ISBN 0 87868 349 6
Short and highly readable account of the foster care system, primarily intended to increase foster carers' understanding of the position of birth parents.

276 LEVIN AE (1992) 'Groupwork with parents in the family foster care system: a powerful method of engagement' *Child Welfare* 71, 5, 457-473
Account of group work with parents, mainly substance abusers, and of the ways in which the group experience may assist them to resume the care of their children.

277 MACDONALD GD (1992) 'Accepting parental responsibility: "future questioning" as a means to avoid foster home placements of children' *Child Welfare* 71, 1, 3-17
Illustration of a family work technique which encourages family members to hypothesise about the future, mapping events and thus potentially altering them. Application of a practice method described by PENN P (1985) 'Feed-forward: future questions, future maps' in *Family Process* 24, 3, reprinted in *Child Welfare* 71, 1, 19-35.

278 *MARSH P (1986) 'Natural families and children in care: an agenda for practice development' *Adoption & Fostering* 10, 4, 20-25 & 19
Paper on the practice implications of research findings on the lack of involvement of families in the lives of their care in care.

279 MONACO M & THOBURN J (1987) *Self-help for parents with children in care* University of East Anglia Social Work Monographs 36pp
ISBN 0 946751 36 6

280 OPPENHEIM L (1992) 'The importance of networks to partnership in child-centred foster care' *Adoption & Fostering* 16, 1, 23-28
Discusses issues of links and contact in terms of networks.

281 SCHATZ MS & BANE W (1991) 'Empowering the parents of children in substitute care: a training model' *Child Welfare* 70, 6, 665-678
Study suggests that group training has positive value for parents.

282 *SINANOGLU P & MALUCCIO AN (eds)(1981) *Parents of children in placement: perspectives and programs* NY: Child Welfare League of America 475pp ISBN 0 87868 181 7
Useful collection of 30 papers, some especially written for this publication, others previously published in a variety of journals and now of classic status.

283 SMITH B (1991) 'Australian women and foster care: a feminist perspective' *Child Welfare* 70, 2, 175-184
Account of one agency's attempt to offer fostering as a form of care in which birth mothers and foster mothers participate.

Foster carers

The response of foster carers, actual and potential, to the demands of the 1989 Act must be a subject for research before long. THOBURN 319 offers a helpful interim discussion. For carers themselves, the obvious starting point is the NFCA's Signpost series.

284 *BEBBINGTON A & MILES J (1990) 'The supply of foster families for children in care' *British Journal of Social Work* 20, 4, 283-307
Comparative study of 2694 foster homes compared with families in the General Household Survey, with an attempt to estimate likely availability in different areas. Confirms social workers' experience that foster homes are most available where they are least needed.

285 BLUNDEN G (1988) 'Becoming a single foster parent' *Adoption & Fostering* 12, 1, 44-47
Describing her personal experience of assessment and training, and her discomfort over social workers' hidden agenda, writer calls for greater openness in dealing with applicants.

286 BROWN HC (1991) 'Competent child-focused practice: working with lesbian and gay carers' *Adoption & Fostering* 15, 2, 11-17
Article outlining the political context and research background for practice in a controversial area of child placement, with some useful further references.

287 CARBINO R (1991) 'Advocacy for foster families in the United States facing child abuse allegations: how social agencies and foster parents are responding to the problem' *Child Welfare* 70, 2, 131-149
Report of a national survey in 1989 indicating little awareness by agencies of the issues for carers and recomending specific changes in policy and procedures.

288 *CAUTLEY PW (1980) *New foster parents: the first experience* NY: Human Sciences Press 287pp ISBN 0 87705 495 9
US study following carers through their first 18 months and suggesting indicators of successful fostering, including familiarity with children, good parenting models from own childhood, willingness to work with social worker and agency, and verbal evidence of parenting skills as applied to specific incidents. Foster fathers emerged as particularly important in determining the likely success of the placement.

289 CORSER AS & FURNELL JRG (1992) 'What do foster parents think of the natural parents? a comparative study' *Child Care Health and*

Development 18, 2, 67-80
Study showing significant differences between short-term carers, social
workers and parents in the general population in attitudes to issues around
admission to care, contact with birth parents, and rehabilitation of abused
children. Implications for recruitment, training and support are discussed.

290 DANDO I & MINTY B (1987) 'What makes good foster parents?' *British
Journal of Social Work* 17, 383-400
Research study suggesting effective fostering is associated with motivation
based on or derived from strong personal needs, eg. childlessness or
experience of deprivation in childhood. Carers expressing altruistic motives
also did well.

291 DOELLING JL & JOHNSON JH (1990) 'Predicting success in foster
placement: the contribution of parent-child temperament characteristics'
American Journal of Orthopsychiatry 60, 585-593
Matching of 'rigid' foster mother with 'negative' child, and placing of a
child with a more negative mood than foster mother expected were
predictive of less successful placement.

292 FULLERTON M (1982) 'A study of the role of foster parents in family
placement for adolescents' *Clearing house for local authority social
services research* 4, 45-138 University of Birmingham Department of
Social Administration
Comparative study of two groups of foster carers – 'traditional' and
'professional' – suggesting that the latter gained more satisfaction from a
sense of carrying out a professional task and looked less for responsiveness
and emotional gratification from the child.

293 LAYCOCK F, THORLEY J & SCHATZBERGER R (1987) 'A team
approach to foster parent assessment' *Adoption & Fostering* 11, 4, 36-37
Describes a way of overcoming the limitations of assessment by one
worker by using a team approach, employing a family therapy model.

294 MALOS E (1991) 'Custodianship: relatives as carers and social worker
assessments' *Adoption & Fostering* 15, 2, 28-33
Article derived from the Custodianship Research Project which contains
lessons for placement with relatives following the Children Act.

295 MARTIN G (1993) 'Foster care: the protection and training of carers'
children' *Child Abuse Review* 2, 15-22
Account of a project for own children of carers who foster abused children.

296 MASTERS B (1990) *Gary* Jonathan Cape 157pp ISBN 0 224 02727 1
Personal account by foster father of a disturbed and violent teenager.

297   MEEZAN W & SHIREMAN JF (1985) *Care and commitment: foster parent adoption decisions* NY: State University 247pp ISBN 88706 104 4
Chicago research into the differences between foster parents who chose to adopt their foster children and those who did not. Interesting incidental finding that foster/adoptive parents were better than social workers at predicting placement outcome.

298   MILLER B (1986) *Room for one more: surviving as a foster mum* John Murray/NFCA 128pp ISBN 0 7195 4342 8
Account of the experiences of a foster mother, by one of the survivors.

299   NFCA (1988) *Child abuse: accusations against foster parents* NFCA 15pp ISBN 0 9460 1550 3

300   NFCA (1990) *A problem shared – a practical approach to difficult foster placements* NFCA 191pp ISBN 0 946015 75 9
Training course in workbook form for groups of carers.

**NFCA Signposts series:
301   (1990) *Managing behaviour – controlling with care* 11pp
302   (1991) *The Children Act 1989* 14pp
303   (1991) *Foster care placements – regulations and guidance* 11pp
304   (1991) *The social worker's visit* 6pp
305   (1991) *Young people and drugs* 13pp
306   (1991) *Social security for young people* 11pp
307   (1992) *Going to court* 7pp
308   (1993) *AIDS and HIV – information for foster carers* 11pp
309   (1993) *Dealing with fostering breakdown* 8pp
310   (1993) *Insurance and foster care* NFCA 11pp
A selection from the National Foster Care Association's Signpost series – regularly added to and updated – offering useful information in concise, readable form, addressed primarily to carers but a handy reference for others also.

311   PART D (1993) 'Fostering as seen by carers' children' *Adoption & Fostering* 17,1, 26-31
Scottish research study.

312   RHODES P (1993) 'Charitable vocation or "proper job"? The role of payment in foster care' *Adoption & Fostering* 17, 1, 8-13
Discussion of issues surrounding demands for fostering to become a salaried service.

313   ROBINSON J (1991) 'Beyond the frontiers of fostering – the employment

of a "professional carer"' *Adoption & Fostering* 15,1 47-49
Account of the employment of a salaried carer in Greenwich.

314   ROCHE E & DUNNE A (1986) *Children in long-term foster care: the
impact of the placement upon twenty foster families* Barnardo's North East
Division 32pp
Exploratory and descriptive study of foster parents' reactions to various
stages of foster care, from assessment to the impact of the placement on
the foster family.

315   ROWE J, CAIN H, HUNDLEBY M & KEANE A (1984) *Long-term
fostering and the Children Act: a study of foster parents who went on to
adopt* BAAF 34pp
Study indicating that an adoption order did not seem to make much
difference to birth parent–child contact: in most cases it had either ceased
long before or continued despite the adoption. Social workers considered
foster parents who adopted to be more likely than those who did not to be
open with the child about origins.

316   RUSHTON A (1989) 'Post-placement services for foster and adoptive
parents: support, counselling or therapy?' *Journal of Child Psychology and
Psychiatry* 30, 2, 197-204
Looks at the range of emotional and behavioural difficulties encountered
by carers and their needs for training and support services.

317   SHAW M (1986) 'Substitute parenting' in W Sluckin & M Herbert (eds)
Parental behaviour Basil Blackwell ISBN 0 631 13487 5
Review of research literature on parenting behaviour in foster and adoptive
parents.

318   SHAW M & HIPGRAVE T (1989) 'Young people and their carers in
specialist fostering' *Adoption & Fostering* 13, 4, 11-17

319   *THOBURN J (1991) 'Permanent family placement and the Children Act
1989: implications for foster carers and social workers' *Adoption &
Fostering* 15, 3, 15-20
Article looking ahead to the Children Act and discussing the future of
permanent placement in relation to partnership with parents and the greater
emphasis on negotiated agreements and reunification with the family.

Foster children

The literature on foster children focuses largely on those seen as having
'special needs', though the label might be thought to apply to any child

looked after by a local authority. Growing concern over parent–child contact is reflected in a separate section, 387-392.

320   BANKS N (1992) 'Techniques for direct identity work with Black children' *Adoption & Fostering* 16, 3, 19-25
Article outlining ways in which social workers and carers can better understand and meet the identity needs of Black children.

321   BUCHANAN A (1993) 'Life under the Children Act 1989' *Adoption & Fostering* 17, 3, 35-38
Account of a project to obtain the reactions of young people in foster or residential homes in three local authorities.

322   FANSHEL D & SHINN EB (1978) *Children in foster care: a longitudinal investigation* NY: Columbia University Press 520pp ISBN 0 231 03576 4
Major New York study whose findings stressed the significance of parent–child contact for reunification and for children's wellbeing in care.

323   FESTINGER T (1983) *No one ever asked us...a postscript to foster care* NY: Columbia University Press 343pp ISBN 0 231 05736 9
New York study of young people who had spent at least five years in care and were aged 18-21 on discharge.

324   HARPER J (1988) 'The inner world of children separated from their parents' *Adoption & Fostering* 12, 1, 14-19

325   HARPER J (1990) 'Children's communication of anxiety through metaphor in fostering and adoption' *Adoption & Fostering* 14, 3, 33-37
Discussion with case illustrations.

326   HICKS C & NIXON S (1989) 'The use of a modified repertory grid technique for assessing the self-concept of children in local authority foster care' *British Journal of Social Work* 19, 3, 203-216
Research study indicating that children in care have lower self-esteem and fewer positive constructs about themselves than children in their own homes. Implications for practice and the use of the repertory grid technique in assessment are discussed.

327   KAHAN B (1979) *Growing up in care: ten people talking* Basil Blackwell 201pp ISBN 0 631 12161 7
Record of group discussions with young adults who grew up in care.

328   MARSHAL K (1991) 'The foster child: the forgotten party?' *Adoption & Fostering* 15, 3, 20-25
Advocates treating children as people rather than as pawns in adult games.

329   PALMER SE (1990) 'Group treatment of foster children to reduce
       separation conflicts associated with placement breakdown' *Child Welfare*
       69, 3, 227-238
       Groupwork project with children aged 7-16 had positive results and
       revealed gaps in agency practice with children and parents.

330   VICKERS D (1993) *Tough love* Children's Society 98pp ISBN 907324
       66 5
       Autobiography of a foster child, a remarkable tribute to the resilience of
       both child and foster carers.

331   WULCAYN F (1991) 'Caseload dynamics and foster care re-entry' *Social
       Service Review* 65, 133-156
       Study to examine how, if at all, children's re-entry to care affects caseload
       dynamics; and to determine whether particular child characteristics were
       associated with return to care.

Children with 'special needs'

332   BORLAND M, O'HARA G & TRISELIOTIS J (1991) 'Placement
       outcomes for children with special needs' *Adoption & Fostering* 15, 2,
       18-28
       Account of a research study of children in permanent family placements,
       showing an 80% success rate, with discussion of factors contributing to
       stability or disruption of placement.

333   EDWARDS K (1989) *Assessment of families for specialist family
       placement: report of a Personal Social Services Fellowship June
       1985–February 1986* University of Bristol Papers in Applied Social Studies
       82pp 0 86292 317 4

334   FANSHEL D, FINCH SJ & GRUNDY JF (1989) 'Foster children in
       life-course perspective: the Casey Family Program experience' *Child
       Welfare* 68, 467-478.
       Article presenting summary findings of Fanshel 335, shorn of
       methodological detail.

335   FANSHEL D, FINCH SJ & GRUNDY JF (1990) *Foster children in a life
       course perspective* Columbia University Press 352pp ISBN 0 231 07180 9
       Research study of 585 children and young people in specialist fostering in
       a US agency, which seeks to explore the persistence of particular events
       and reactions to them over the 'life-course' of the child. Quite heavily
       statistical but some useful, if necessarily complex, discussion.

336   FLUX M et al (1987) 'Conjoint assessment of families and children'

Adoption & Fostering 11, 3, 39-43
Describes a method of assessing families and children together, which has improved the chances of a placement being made for children with severe emotional disturbance or disabilities.

337   *FRATTER J, ROWE J, SAPSFORD D & THOBURN J (1991) *Permanent family placement: a decade of experience* BAAF Research series 125pp ISBN 0 903534 96 7
Account of a research study of 1,165 children with special needs placed by voluntary agencies 1980-84, with discussion of policy and practice implications.

338   *GALAWAY B, MAGLAJLIC D, HUDSON J, HARMON P & McLAGAN J (1990) *International perspectives on specialist foster family care* Minnesota: Human Services Associates 203pp. ISBN 0 8087 5153 0
Sixteen short papers including a couple of contributions from the UK.

339   HAWKINS RP & BREILING J (1989) *Therapeutic foster care: critical issues* Washington DC: Child Welfare League of America 221pp ISBN 0 87868 355 0
Presents the results of a US study of therapeutic foster care programmes and offers a range of contributions on training and supervision, the involvement of birth parents, and likely future developments in this area of foster care.

340   HILL M, NUTTER R, GILTINAN D, HUDSON J & GALAWAY B (1993) 'A comparative survey of specialist fostering in the UK and North America' *Adoption & Fostering* 17, 2, 17-22

341   HUDSON J, GALAWAY B (eds)(1989) *Specialist foster family care: a normalizing experience* NY & London: Haworth Press 275pp ISBN 0 86656 939 1
Papers on the development of specialist fostering in the USA, Canada and the UK covering a broad range of policy, organisational and practice issues.

342   HUNTER A (1989) *Family placement: models of effective partnership* Ilford: Barnardo's Practice Paper 130pp ISBN 0 902046 01 2
Practice discussion of the family placement process drawing on the experience of various Barnardo schemes.

343   OWEN L (1989) *Professional foster care: a client perspective study* University of East Anglia Social Work Monograph 32pp 0 946751 57 9
Study derived from interviews with young people placed via a specialist fostering scheme.

344   SHAW M & HIPGRAVE T (1983) *Specialist fostering* Batsford/BAAF
152pp ISBN 0 7134 1987 3
Account of two research studies – one local, one national – followed by
discussion of policy and practice issues in specialist fostering.

345   SHAW M & HIPGRAVE T (1989) 'Specialist fostering 1988 – a research
study' *Adoption & Fostering*, 13, 3, 17-21
Update on 1983 work showing considerable spread of specialist fostering
schemes throughout the UK but also emerging problems, often linked to
under-resourcing. See also 318.

346   WESTACOTT J (1988) *Bridge to calmer waters – a study of a Bridge
Families Scheme* Ilford: Barnardo's 99pp ISBN x 10 299405 5
Account of a model of specialist fostering for the middle age-range child,
providing preparation for a new permanent placement and assessment after
a placement disruption.

Older children

347   **ALDGATE J, MALUCCIO A & REEVES C (ed) (1989) *Adolescents
in foster families* Batsford/BAAF 192pp ISBN 0 7134 6014 8
Range of papers on issues relating to selection, preparation and support of
young people and foster families.

348   ALDGATE J (1989) 'Foster families and residential care for older children:
some interpersonal dynamics' *Children & Society* 3, 1, 12-36
Using an ecological perspective, the author discusses the value of
residential care for some older children, and argues the need for a
comprehensive assessment and for listening to consumer views.

349   *DOWNES C (1982) 'How endings are experienced in time-limited family
placement of difficult adolescents' *Journal of Adolescence* 5, Dec, 379-394.
Author identifies four patterns of reaction by teenagers and their carers to
the prospect of the placement coming to an end, and discusses implications
for practice.

350   *DOWNES C (1982) 'Assessing adolescents for time-limited foster care'
Adoption & Fostering 6, 4, 26-30 & 53
Emphasises importance for the adolescent of being seen in the context of
existing attachments, and being given opportunities to find and use adults
outside the formal caring network.

351   DOWNES C (1987) 'Fostered teenagers and children in the family'
Adoption & Fostering 11, 4, 11-16
Report of a study of interactions between fostered teenagers and children

of the family. Author notes some disturbing findings with implications for practice.

352 *DOWNES C (1988) 'Foster families for adolescents: the healing potential of time-limited placements' *British Journal of Social Work* 18, 473-487

353 DOWNES C (1990) 'Security and autonomy: criteria for judging the quality of care offered to adolescents in time-limited placements' in S Baldwin, C Godfrey & C Propper (eds) *Quality of life: perspectives and policies* Routledge ISBN 0 415 09581 6

354 **HAZEL N (1981) *A bridge to independence: the Kent Family Placement Project* Basil Blackwell 175pp ISBN 0 631 12943 X
Account of the pioneer project which was to become the model for most specialist fostering throughout the UK.

355 NFCA (1985) *Teenagers in care – seminars on fostering adolescents* NFCA 73pp

356 NFCA (1990) *Teenagers in foster care: a survey by the National Foster Care Association* NFCA 68pp
Survey showing wide variation in services throughout the UK.

357 O'HARA G & DEWAR C (1988) 'Fostering teenagers – what works for whom and why?' *Adoption & Fostering* 12, 2, 38-43
Findings from work undertaken in Lothian.

358 PROCH K & TABER MA (1987) 'Alienated adolescents in foster care' *Social Work Research and Abstracts* 23, 2, 9-13
US study focusing on interactions between young person and carer as significant factors in placement disruption, pattern reflecting alienation and mutual rejection.

Children with medical conditions and disabilities

359 BAAF *The placement of children with disabilities* BAAF Practice Note 22
Concerned mainly with children with severe to profound physical and mental disabilities.

360 BATTY D (1987) (ed) *The implications of AIDS for children in care* BAAF 84pp ISBN 0 903534 72 X
Collection of papers on AIDS and child placement implications.

361 *BATTY D (ed) (1993) *HIV infection and children in need* BAAF 150pp ISBN 1 873868 08 1

A range of papers on the nature of HIV and AIDS and the care and placement of children who are affected. Updates 360.

362 CURTIS S (ed) (1987) *From asthma to thalassaemia: medical conditions in childhood* BAAF 160pp ISBN 0 903534 69 X
Information on a wide range of conditions and their implications for the care of children who are affected.

363 DIXON N, FLANAGAN R, HARDY J, KERMODE S, DODSON L & SPENCER C (1987) *Special fostering: fostering children and young people who are mentally handicapped* Barnardo Practice Papers 113pp ISBN X 10 173240 5
Report on a project to find suitable foster homes. Each stage of the process was evaluated, with feedback from carers.

364 HART G (1987) 'Placing children with AIDS' *Adoption & Fostering* 11, 1, 41-43
Brief discussion of AIDS and placement implications.

365 **NFCA (1991) *Fostering children with disabilities* NFCA
Booklet offering information and guidance on a range of issues relating to the foster care of children with visual, hearing and learning disabilities.

366 NFCA (1991) *Children with disabilities in foster care: a survey by the National Foster Care Association* NFCA 44pp
Report of a project intended to establish an information and advice service for agencies and carers.

367 RENDON M, GURDIN P, BASSI J & WESTON M (1989) 'Foster care for children with AIDS: a psychosocial perspective' *Child Psychiatry & Human Development* 19, 256-269
US preliminary study of programme for placing babies with AIDS, showing high level of success.

Sibling groups

368 BOER F & SPIERING SM (1991) 'Siblings in foster care: success and failure' *Child Psychiatry & Human Development* 21, 291-300
Retrospective study of sibling placements and factors in disruption.

369 HEGAR RL (1988) 'Sibling relationships and separations: implications for child placement' *Social Service Review* 62, 3, 446-467
Comprehensive review of US research concluding that sibling ties are highly important to many foster children and that these links need greater attention in placement planning.

370   HEGAR RL (1993) 'Assessing attachment, permanence, and kinship in
       choosing permanent homes' *Child Welfare* 72, 4, 367-378
       Author uses a case study involving siblings to demonstrate the importance
       of balancing various factors in placement decisions.

371   MACLEAN K (1991) 'Meeting the needs of sibling groups in care'
       Adoption & Fostering 15, 1, 33-37
       Account of the writer's research, discussion of others' findings in this field,
       and suggestions for improving the chances of successful placement.

372   MORRISON T & BROWN J (1986) 'Splitting siblings' *Adoption &
       Fostering* 10, 4, 47-51
       Case study involving the separate placement of three siblings.

373   RUSHTON A, TRESEDER J & QUINTON D (1989) 'Sibling groups in
       permanent placements' *Adoption & Fostering* 13, 4, 5-11

374   TIMBERLAKE EM & HAMLIN ER (1982) 'The sibling group: a
       neglected dimension of placement' *Child Welfare* 61, 8, 545-552
       Discussion of practice issues, mainly on handling the situation where only
       one member of a sibling group is to be placed.

375   WARD M (1984) 'Sibling ties in foster care and adoption planning' *Child
       Welfare* 63, 4, 321-332
       Discussion of the importance of sibling ties, with recommendations for
       maintaining links throughout the placement process.

Children who have been abused or neglected

376   AUESTAD A (1987) 'The role of the therapist in cases of child
       neglect/maltreatment, with a special focus on foster placement' *Journal
       of Social Work Practice* 3, 1, 4-13

377   *BATTY D (ed) (1991) *Sexually abused children – making their
       placements work* BAAF 128pp ISBN 0 903534 94 0
       Papers discussing a wide range of issues around placement and working
       with children who have been abused; preparation and support of carers;
       and implications for medical and educational services.

378   DAVIS E, KIDD L & PRINGLE K (1987) *Child sexual abuse training
       programme for foster parents with teenage placements* Barnardo's North
       East Division 104pp

379   LIE G & McMURTY SL (1991) 'Foster care for sexually abused children:
       a comparative study' *Child Abuse & Neglect* 15, 1/2, 111-121
       Comparative study of children placed following sexual abuse and a control

group showed similar profiles in terms of behavioural problems and other attributes. But the sexually abused children left foster care more quickly than the non-abused children.

380   *MACASKILL C (1991) *Adopting or fostering a sexually abused child* Batsford/BAAF 173pp ISBN 0 7134 6760 0
Research study of 66 families, with discussion of implications for practice. Not planned as a theoretical textbook, it sets out to convey the day-to-day realities for adoptive and foster families living with children who have been abused.

381   NFCA (1993) *Fostering a child who has been sexually abused* NFCA 14pp
Helpful pamphlet providing information and advice for carers.

382   PRINGLE K (1990) *Managing to survive – developing a resource for sexually abused young people* Barnardo's North East Division 93pp plus appendices
Crisis Assessment Placement Service – evaluation of a pilot project.

383   ROBERTS J (1986) 'Fostering the sexually abused child' *Adoption & Fostering* 10, 1, 8-11
Guidance derived from writer's practice in Lambeth.

384   ROBERTS J (1989) 'Substitute care for abused and neglected children' *Adoption & Fostering* 13, 3, 37-43
Author discusses the particular needs of such children and oulines some methods of meeting these needs and of improving substitute care.

385   ROSENTHAL JA (1991) 'A descriptive study of abuse and neglect in out-of-home placement' *Child Abuse & Neglect* 13,3, 249-260

386   SMITH G (1986) 'Child sexual abuse: the power of intrusion' *Adoption & Fostering* 10, 3, 13-18 Article on sexual abuse followed by contribution from a foster carer looking after a child who has been abused.

Contact

Contact between parents and their children in foster care remains a highly problematic issue, and not only in long-term placements (see WATERHOUSE 392). Growing attention in the literature to ways of promoting and improving the quality of contact is to be warmly welcomed. See also FAMILY RIGHTS GROUP 016.

387   FAMILY RIGHTS GROUP (1986) *Promoting links: keeping children and families in touch* FRG 127pp ISBN x 10 299405 5

Pamphlet containing a range of papers on the importance and problems of maintaining good links.

388   *FAMILY RIGHTS GROUP/NFCA/BAAF (1990) *Maintaining contact – partnership in practice* Training pack Barnardo's

389   **HESS PM & PROCH KO (1993) *Contact: managing visits to children looked after away from home* BAAF 88pp ISBN 1 873868 12 X
Welcome UK version of a US publication offering helpful discussion and guidelines on all aspects of child–parent contact, with particular attention to planning and management.

390   MASSON J (1990) 'Contact between parents and children in long-term care' *International Journal of Law and the Family* 4, 92-113

391   MILLHAM S, BULLOCK R, HOSIE K & LITTLE M (1989) *Access disputes in child care* Aldershot: Gower 110pp ISBN 0 566 07087 1
Research study into situations where local authorities' attempts to end parental contact have been challenged by parents. Findings and discussion still relevant post-1989 Act.

392   *WATERHOUSE S (1992) 'How foster carers view contact' *Adoption & Fostering* 16, 2, 42-47
Article on a research study with discussion of the practice implications following the Children Act.

Reunification, leaving care and aftercare

Historically, much more attention has been given to children entering the care system than to those leaving it. Following the work of STEIN and colleagues in the 1980s, and the higher profile given to leaving care and aftercare in the Children Act 1989 – where they are firmly part of 'looking after' children – these services have received significantly greater attention in the literature. Of recent writing, BULLOCK et al 396 is particularly rewarding and enjoyable to read.

393   BIEHAL M, CLAYDEN J, STEIN M & WADE J (1992) *Prepared for living? a survey of young people leaving the care of three local authorities* National Children's Bureau 45pp

394   BONNERJEA L (1990) *Leaving care in London* London Boroughs Children's Regional Planning Committee 123pp ISBN 1 872951 00 7

395   BRICKMAN AS, DEY S & CUTHBERT P (1991) 'A supervised independent living program for adolescents' *Child Welfare* 70,1, 69-80

Description of a relatively unstructured but supervised independent living programme for young people with a history of behavioural and emotional disturbance.

396   **BULLOCK R, LITTLE M & MILLHAM S (1993) *Going home: the return of children separated from their families* Dartmouth Publishing Co Ltd 263pp ISBN 1 85521 329 X
Another in the excellent series of studies from the Dartington Social Research Unit, derived from a large-scale retrospective study and an intensive prospective study of care-leavers, with predictors for returning home and successful reunification.

397   CHILDREN'S SOCIETY (1992) *The next step: a guide to leaving care* 2nd edition Children's Society 48pp ISBN 0 907324 69 X
Clear, practical guidance addressed to young people on topics such as aftercare services, housing, budgeting, job-hunting, benefits, education, rights, and much more.

398   CHILDREN'S SOCIETY (1992) *Preparing young people for independent living: the Children's Society's Battersea Bedsit Project* Children's Society 72pp ISBN 0 907324 65 7
Report produced by residents and staff.

399   FARMER E & PARKER R (1991) *Trials and tribulations: returning children from local authority care to their families* HMSO 200pp ISBN 0 11 321148 1
Research study into the progress of over 300 children returned to their families following removal in court proceedings. Concludes with proposals for improved service.

400   FARMER E (1992) 'Restoring children on court orders to their families: lessons for practice' *Adoption & Fostering* 16, 1, 7-15 Article derived from 399.

401   FEIN E & STAFF I (1991) 'Implementing reunification services' *Families in Society* 72, 6, 335-343
Account of a family reunification programme with discussion of goal setting, service agreements, abuse in foster families, and burnout.

402   FIRST KEY (1987) *A study of black young people leaving care* London: First Key 15pp
Short but useful account of a study in three London boroughs. Discusses the admission of young black people into the care system, the dangers of loss of identity in care, and the needs of black young people in care.

403   GARNETT L (1992) *Leaving care and after* National Children's Bureau
      132pp + appendix ISBN 0 902 817 79 X
      Study undertaken in three of the Child Care Now local authorities – see 214.

404   GOERGE RM (1990) 'The reunification process in substitute care' *Social
      Service Review* 64, 3, 422-457
      Illinois study showing probability of reunification declines after first few
      weeks of placement; greatest risk of non-return home is for abused and
      neglected children; placements with relatives are the most stable.

405   HESS PM, FOLARON G & JEFFERSON AB (1992) 'Effectiveness of
      family reunification services: an innovative evaluative model' *Social
      Work* 37, 4, 304-311
      Research study which found that the most common factor in children's
      return to care was failure to resolve the parent problem that first led to
      placement. High caseloads, staff turnover and inadequate supervision of
      practice interacted with family problems to reduce the chances of a
      successful return home.

406   *MALUCCIO AN, KRIEGER R & PINE BA (1990) *Preparing
      adolescents for life after foster care: the central role of foster parents*
      Washington DC: Child Welfare League of America 225pp
      ISBN 0 87868 433 6
      Papers by a number of authors on topics such as the psychological
      adjustment of teenagers in foster care, preparation and training of foster
      families, strengths of black foster families, involving birth families, and
      the development of interdependent living programmes.

407   MORGAN C & TAYLOR A (1987) 'A study of black young people leaving
      care' *Social Services Research* University of Birmingham 5/6, 10-24
      Study in three contrasting London boroughs highlighting the need to
      involve the black community in work with black young people leaving
      care; and examine work undertaken for hidden assumptions about leaving
      home on which young people and their workers may be operating.

408   NATIONAL CHILDREN'S BUREAU (1992) *Leaving care* NCB
      Highlight no 107

409   RZEPNICKI TL (1987) 'Recidivism of foster children returned to their
      own homes: a review and new directions for research' *Social Service
      Review* 61, 1, 56-70
      Article reviewing what is known of factors associated with children's
      re-entry into care following return home.

410   SIMMS MD & BOLDEN BJ (1991) 'The Family Reunification Project:

facilitating regular contact among foster children, biological families and foster families' *Child Welfare* 70, 6, 679-690
Account of a 16-week pilot programme of structured contact in a neutral setting, which had encouraging results.

411 **STEIN M & CAREY K (1986) *Leaving care* Batsford 189pp
ISBN 0 631 14875 2
Follow-up study of young people leaving care, vividly illustrating the problems to be faced, and indicating that it is more realistic to prepare them for *interdependent* than for *independent* living.

412 STEIN M (1992) *Living out of care* Ilford: Barnardo's 87pp.

413 STONE M (1990) *Young people leaving care* Royal Philanthropic Society. 96pp ISBN 1 873134 00 2
Study of management systems, service delivery and user evaluation in 39 leaving care schemes.

414 THOBURN J (1980) *Captive clients: social work with families of children home on trial* Routledge & Kegan Paul 202pp ISBN 0 7100 0528 8
Study of children living at home under care or supervision orders. Most important factor in the decision to let the children return or remain at home was the determination of most of the parents and of their children to stay together as a family. Attitudes and skills of the social workers in mobilising necessary resources and the nature of the practical and emotional support offered were also important.

415 TIMBERLAKE EM, PASZTOR E, SHEAGREN J, CLARREN J & LAMMERT M (1987) 'Adolescent emancipation from foster care' *Child and Adolescent Social Work Journal* 4, 264-277
Demonstration project involving 31 teenagers moving from foster care to semi-independent living, produced improvements in various skills, though not in psycho-social functioning. Note the use in much US literature of the term 'emancipation', defined in the OED as setting free from slavery or, more generally, from civil disabilities.

416 TRENT J (1989) *Homeward bound: the rehabilitation of children to their birth parents* Barnardo's New Families Project, Colchester 102pp

4 Adoption

At the time of writing, the UK adoption world awaits legislation to bring law, policy and practice into line with the Children Act 1989. Radical change is nothing new in adoption. Only a few decades ago, the emphasis in the literature was on work with unmarried mothers (rarely fathers), the timing and appropriateness of their consent to adoption, the care and assessment of babies as to their suitability for adoption, the quest for the ideal adoptive couple, and the careful 'matching' of baby and adoptive applicants.

From around 1970, with fewer newborn babies being offered for adoption, the focus moved to the placement of older children with an identifiable family of origin, a wide range of moderate to serious disabilities, and sometimes lengthy experience of hospital or local authority care. This involved a long-overdue switch from the interests of adopters to the interests of children but resulted in a dangerously partial view of permanency planning which led in some quarters to an over-enthusiasm for adoption and an imbalance which the Children Act seeks to redress.

General

Some recent literature blurs the distinctions between adoption and foster family care, referring broadly to 'permanent family placement'. There is thus some overlap between this and the preceding chapter. BEAN 423 and BRODZINSKY & SCHECHTER 426 provide the best theoretical introductions; while KING 436 and LINDSAY & MONSERRAT 438 are addressed to a more popular market.

417   ADAMEC C & PIERCE WL (1991) *The encyclopedia of adoption* NY & Oxford: Facts on File 382pp ISBN 0 8160 2108 2
      Short entries on numerous topics alphabetically arranged, somehow less

useful than first sight suggests. UK readers will be sceptical of any adoption 'encyclopedia' which fails to include BAAF or *Adoption & Fostering.*

418   BAAF (1992) *Adoption – some questions answered*

419   BAAF (1992) *Stepchildren and adoption (England and Wales)*

420   BAAF (1992) *Stepchildren and adoption (Scotland)*
Series of informative and well-designed leaflets for the general public. Others specifically intended for birth parents, adopters and children are noted under the appropriate sections below.

421   BAAF *Social work reports in Adoption Proceedings* (Scotland)
BAAF Practice Note 19

422   BARTH RP, BERRY M, YOSHIKAMI R GOODFIELD RK & CARSON ML (1988) 'Predicting adoption disruption' *Social Work* 33, 3, 227-233
Californian study 1980-84 noting a decline in the rate of disruption over that period to 10%, largely attributed to greater use of foster parents as adopters. Placements of siblings together were not especially likely to disrupt; transracial placements no more likely than others to disrupt; older children and those with previous adoption placements were most at risk of disruption.

423   **BEAN P (ed) (1984) *Adoption: essays in social policy, law and sociology* Tavistock 313pp ISBN 0 422 79410 9
Eighteen papers on a range of issues including older child adoption, causes and treatment of behaviour problems, a review of research on children growing up adopted, the role of voluntary agencies, obtaining birth certificates, subsidised adoption, and a contribution from an adoptive couple. There are several papers on legal issues and transracial adoption.

424   BENET MK (1976) *The character of adoption* Jonathan Cape 237pp ISBN 0 224 01199 5
A historical and cross-cultural perspective on key issues in contemporary Western adoption, with some fascinating material on adoption in other times and places.

425   BRINICH P (1990) 'Adoption, ambivalence and mourning: clinical and theoretical interrelationships' *Adoption & Fostering* 14, 1, 6-16

426   **BRODZINSKY DM & SCHECHTER MD (eds)(1990) *Psychology of adoption* Oxford University Press 396pp ISBN 0 19 504892 X
Collection of papers on theoretical perspectives, adjustment, research, clinical issues, and social policy and casework issues in adoption.

427 **CHENNELLS P & HAMMOND C (1990) *Adopting a child: a guide for people interested in adoption* BAAF 48pp ISBN 0 903534 91 6

428 CULLEN D & WHITE J (1992) 'Adoption Law Review – checklist of changes' *Adoption & Fostering* 16, 4, 7-11
Summary of proposed major changes and implications for practice.

DEPARTMENT OF HEALTH (1990) Discussion papers produced for the Inter-Departmental Review of Adoption Law:

429 1 *The nature and effect of adoption*

430 2 *Review of research relating to adoption* (by June Thoburn)

431 3 *International perspectives* (by Ellen France)

432 DEPARTMENT OF HEALTH (1992) *Review of Adoption Law: report to ministers of an inter-departmental working group* ISBN X 75 189484 1

433 DEPARTMENT OF HEALTH/WELSH OFFICE/HOME OFFICE/LORD CHANCELLOR'S DEPARTMENT (1993) *Adoption: the future* Cm 2288 HMSO ISBN 0 10 122882 1
White Paper on proposed adoption legislation.

434 HILL M (1991) 'Concepts of parenthood and their application to adoption' *Adoption & Fostering* 15, 4, 16-23
Discusses various dimensions of parenthood and their relevance to our understanding of adoption.

435 HUMPHREY M & HUMPHREY H (1988) *Families with a difference: varieties of surrogate parenthood* Routledge 225pp ISBN 415 00690 2
Discusses the growing range of 'alternative' family forms including step-parenting, fostering, adoption, parenthood by donor insemination, *in vitro* fertilisation and surrogacy. A recurrent theme is whether, when and what to tell the children.

436 **KING A (1989) *Adoption and fostering: a practical guide* Marlborough, Wilts: Crowood Press 159pp ISBN 1 85223 133 5
Written in popular style and addressed to anyone considering adoption or fostering.

437 KIRK HD (1985) *Adoptive kinship: a modern institution in need of reform* 2nd edition Ben-Simon Publications 200pp ISBN 0 914539 01 9
Interesting blend of social science and personal biography in which the writer seeks to broaden the analysis developed in *Shared fate* (see 547) into consideration of adoption as a social institution.

438   LINDSAY J & MONSERRAT C (1989) *Adoption awareness: a guide for teachers, counsellors, nurses and caring others* California: Morning Glory Press 286pp ISBN 0 930934 32 6
Guidance for anyone likely to come in contact with adoption.

439   MACINTYRE JE (1989) 'Adoption disruption: recent studies in the US and Canada' *Adoption & Fostering* 13, 4, 31-35

440   MASSON J, NORBURY D & CHATTERTON SG (1983) *Mine, yours or ours? a study of step-parent adoption* HMSO 130pp ISBN 0 11 320835 9
Study in three local authority areas, revealing substantial variations in legal and social work practices.

441   McROY RG, GROTEVANT HD, LOPEZ SA & FURUTA A (1990) 'Adoption revelation and communication issues: implications for practice' *Families in Society* 71, 9, 550-557
Article derived from study of adopted adolescents receiving residential treament, offering a guide for assessing communication problems and interventive methods.

442   MELINA LR (1987) *Adoption: an annotated bibliography and guide* NY: Garland 292pp ISBN 0 8240 8942 1
With 845 references and comments, this will be appreciated by anyone needing a fully comprehensive guide.

443   MURCH M, LOWE N, BORKOWSKI M, COPNER R & GRIEW K (1993) *Pathways to adoption research project* Department of Health/ HMSO 288pp ISBN 0 11 321588 6
Study by the Socio-Legal Centre for Family Studies at Bristol University.

444   REICH D & BATTY D (1990) *The adoption triangle* training pack BAAF ISBN 0 903534 90 8
Designed for adoption workers and staff in related agencies and disciplines involved in any aspect of adoption work. The trainer's guide and the participants' workbooks are also available separately.

445   REICH D (1992) 'Adoption and the story-teller' *Adoption & Fostering* 16, 4, 11-14
Adoption as interpreted in four contemporary novels.

446   RICHARDS J (1993) 'Adoption law review – some views from the triangle' *Adoption & Fostering* 17, 1, 40-43
Short account of views of adopted people, birth parents and adopters on the adoption process.

447   RYBURN M (1992) 'Contested adoption proceedings' *Adoption &*

Fostering 16, 4, 29-38
Account of the experiences of 12 families.

448   RYBURN M (1993) 'The effects of an adversarial process on adoption
      proceedings' *Adoption & Fostering* 17, 3, 39-45
      Paper arguing for the abolition of freeing procedures and the dispensing
      with parental agreement in adoption proceedings as being contrary to the
      spirit of the Children Act.

449   SOCIAL SERVICES INSPECTORATE (undated – 1992/3) *Planning for
      permanence? Adoption services in 3 Northern local authorities* Department
      of Health 81pp + appendices

450   TANSEY BJ (ed) (1988) *Exploring adoptive family life: the collected
      adoption papers of H David Kirk* Washington & British Columbia:
      Ben-Simon Publ 275pp ISBN 0 914539 03 5

451   TEAGUE A (1989) *Social change, social work and the adoption of children*
      Avebury Publ 147pp ISBN 0566070561
      Historical and sociological analysis of the development of adoption
      legislation in the UK.

452   TEXTOR MR (1992) 'Adoptions in West Germany: attitudes of social
      workers' *British Journal of Social Work* 22, 5, 551-564

453   TRISELIOTIS J (1989) 'Some moral and practical issues in adoption work'
      Adoption & Fostering 13, 2, 21-27
      Article examining problems which arise when practice is based on fashion
      or ignorance rather than on empirical knowledge and ethical considerations.

454   VERDIER P (1988) 'Limited adoption in France' *Adoption & Fostering*
      12, 1, 41-44

455   WINKLER RC, BROWN DW, KEPPEL MV & BLANCHARD A (1988)
      Clinical practice in adoption Pergamon Press 138pp ISBN 0 08 034222 1
      Primarily for psychologists and related practitioners, offering a life-course
      perspective, with material on clinical issues and methods, the experience
      of birth parents, adopters and adopted people, special needs, surrogacy,
      AID, transracial and open adoption.

Open adoption

The move from 'closed' to 'semi-open' adoption – from a position of
no communication between birth and adoptive parents to brief
pre-adoption contact – took place gradually in the UK over about 20-25

years. The progression from 'semi-open' to fully 'open' adoption (with occasional post-adoption exchanges of letters and even visits) has been achieved over a much shorter period – the first edition of this bibliography, for example, had no separate section on this topic. The trend has clearly been accelerated by the increase in adoptions of older children, including those with a history of local authority or voluntary agency care.

Like much received wisdom throughout the history of adoption, enthusiasm for 'openness' appears driven more by ideology than by empirical evidence of its benefits. There is some evidence that it can be helpful to the adults involved; its value for children (particularly those placed in infancy) has yet to be demonstrated. More child-focused follow-up research is clearly needed but the best starting-point for the moment is the collection of papers in MULLENDER 467.

US writers lagged behind in this debate through much of the 1970s and 1980s, earnestly debating the 'sealed record controversy' long after the 'search for origins' had been officially recognised in this country. All the more surprising, then, is the recent flood of US journal articles and books (usually) extolling the merits of open adoption and advocating this mode of adoption above all others. When the experts are so agreed, it is perhaps time for caution!

456 *BERRY M (1991) 'The effects of open adoption on biological and adoptive parents and the children: the arguments and evidence' *Child Welfare* 70, 6, 637-651
Author argues that biological parents are the main beneficiaries of open adoption, children more at risk because of their limited ability to understand their various relationships.

457 BLANTON TL & DESCHNER J (1990) 'Biological mothers' grief: the postadoptive experience in open versus confidential adoption' *Child Welfare* 69, 6, 525-535
Limited study suggests that it may be more difficult in open than in closed adoption for birth mothers to come to terms with the loss of their children.

458 CORCORAN A (1988) 'Open adoption: the child's right' *Adoption & Fostering* 12, 3, 39-41

459 DUTT R & SANYAL A (1991) '"Openness" in adoption or open adoption – a black perspective' *Adoption & Fostering* 15, 4, 111-115

Article advocating, amongst other things, greater openness in work with black children and families.

460   ETTER J (1993) 'Levels of co-operation and satisfaction in 56 open adoptions' *Child Welfare* 72, 3, 257-267
Follow-up several years after adoption found high levels of compliance and satisfaction with post-adoption contact agreements.

461   FRATTER J (1991) 'Parties in the triangle' *Adoption & Fostering* 15, 4, 91-98
Article derived from a study indicating advantages in greater openness and maintenance of links after adoption.

462   GRITTER JL (ed) (1989) *Adoption without fear* San Antonio: Corona Publishing Co 171pp ISBN 0 931722 71 3
Short accounts by birth and adoptive parents of their experiences of open adoption.

463   *GROSS HE (1993) 'Open adoption: a research-based literature review and new data' *Child Welfare* 72, 3, 269-284
A review of six previous studies and some new material supporting cautious optimism on birth and adoptive parents' responses to open adoption.

464   KANUIK J (1991) 'Parental responsibility and open attitudes in adoption' *Adoption & Fostering* 15,3, 34-39
Discusses likely developments in the adoption field in the light of the Children Act.

465   LINDSAY JW (1987) *Open adoption: a caring option* California: Morning Glory Press 254pp ISBN 0 930934 23 7
Popular-style guide to open adoption.

466   McROY RG (1991) 'American experience and research on openness' *Adoption & Fostering* 15, 4, 99-111
Review of US studies on open adoption and analysis of degrees of openness which may be appropriate in different circumstances.

467   *MULLENDER A (1991)(ed) *Open adoption: the philosophy and the practice* BAAF 162pp ISBN 0 903534 95 9
Contributions from professionals and from people personally involved in the adoption process.

468   ROMPF EL (1993) 'Open adoption: what does the "average person" think?' *Child Welfare* 72, 3, 219-230
US study found the general public generally sympathetic to the idea of open adoption.

469   RYBURN M (1990) 'Openness in adoption' *Adoption & Fostering* 14, 1, 21-26
        Article drawing on New Zealand adoption experience.

470   SIEGEL DH (1993) 'Open adoption of infants: adoptive parents' perceptions of advantages and disadvantages' *Social Work* 38, 1, 15-23
        US agency research study showing largely positive reactions of adopters to open adoption experience.

471   TRISELIOTIS J (1991) 'Maintaining the links in adoption' *British Journal of Social Work* 21, 401-414
        Review of various researches which concludes that, provided contact is handled constructively and positively, there is no evidence of damage to the child through divided loyalties etc.

Ethnic issues in adoption

The professional literature (sadly, not politicians or the press) has moved on from the position noted in the first edition whereby 'ethnic issues' was almost synonymous with 'transracial adoption'. In addition to the more general materials listed in this section, relevant titles will be found under Intercountry Adoption 650-661 and throughout most of the following sections. Items primarily concerned with the transracial placement debate are to be found in the next section, 480-492.

472   BAAF *Recruiting Black Families* BAAF Practice Note 18

473   BRUNTON L & WELCH M (1983) 'White agency, black community' *Adoption & Fostering* 7, 2, 16-18
        Account of a recruitment campaign, acknowledging the impact of institutional racism and arguing that problems in finding black families lie not in their reluctance to come forward but in agencies' reluctance to accept what is being offered.

474   COMMISSION FOR RACIAL EQUALITY (1990) *Adopting a better policy: adoption and fostering of ethnic minority children – the race dimension* CRE

475   DAY D (1979) *The adoption of black children: counteracting institutional discrimination* Mass: Lexington Books 156pp ISBN 0 669 02107 5
        Strong attack on racism in social work practice, with a useful section on interaction between white workers and black clients, and ways of overcoming communication barriers.

476   KANIUK J (1990) 'Strategies in recruiting black adopters' *Adoption &*
        Fostering 15, 1, 38-42
        Based on author's experience at Thomas Coram, discussion of strategies
        under three headings – staffing and staff awareness, communication with
        the black community and developing a responsive and sensitive service to
        black applicants.

477   RODRIGUEZ P & MEYER AS (1990) 'Minority adoptions and agency
        practices' *Social Work* 35, 6, 528-531
        US study showing how some agencies are able to attract applicants from
        ethnic minorities, though problems remain in achieving placement for older
        children and those with serious disabilities.

478   ROSENTHAL JA, GROZE V & CURIEL H (1990) 'Race, social class,
        and special needs adoption' *Social Work* 35, 6, 532-539
        US study in which ethnic minority parents, low-income and less
        well-educated adopters reported more positive relationships with their
        children.

479   SANDVEN K & RESNICK MD (1990) 'Informal adoption among black
        adolescent mothers' *American Journal of Orthopsychiatry* 60, 210-214
        US study of 'informal' adoption by 54 black teenage mothers.

Transracial adoption

In the absence of strong research evidence either way on the long-term
consequences of transracial placement, the debate continues largely at
an ideological level. Such empirical evidence as there is suggests a less
damaging outcome for transracial placements than might be feared. But
there remain nagging doubts as to the sensitivity of research instruments
in exploring issues such as identity.

480   BAGLEY C (1993) 'Transracial adoption in Britain: a follow-up study,
        with policy considerations' *Child Welfare* 72, 3, 285-299
        Follow-up study at age 19 of African-Caribbean and mixed-parentage
        children placed transracially. Variety of tests gave generally excellent
        results. No evidence that intercultural identity led to unfavourable
        adjustment. The young people seemed well prepared to participate
        effectively in a multicultural and multiracial society. Author recommends
        transracial adoption for any child who cannot be placed inracially.

481   DALE D (1987) *Denying homes to black children: Britain's new race*
        adoption policies Social Affairs Unit 38pp ISBN 0 907631 23 1
        Controversial pamphlet claiming that black children are condemned to

institutional care because of doctrinaire opposition to transracial family placement. Author argues that opposition stems from political ideology rather than from proper evaluation of available research evidence.

482   FEIGELMAN W & SILVERMAN AR (1984) 'The long-term effects of transracial adoption' *Social Service Review* 58, 4, 588-602
Follow-up after six years in placement finds no evidence to support critical attack on transracial adoption – children doing as well as their peers in same-race adoption.

483   GILL O & JACKSON B (1983) *Adoption and race: black, Asian and mixed race children in white families* Batsford/BAAF 151pp ISBN 0 7134 20235
UK follow-up study of children placed transracially in the 1960s. On various indicators, the children have done well, but questions are raised as to their sense of ethnic identity.

484   GROW LJ & SHAPIRO D (1974) *Black children, white parents: a study of transracial adoption* NY: Child Welfare League of America 239pp ISBN 0 87868 152 3
Early US study of 125 transracially-placed children concluded that most were doing well, but a substantial minority of families were 'in serious trouble'.

485   HARRIS K (1985) *Transracial adoption – a bibliography* BAAF 122pp ISBN 0 903534 59 2
Annotated bibliography of 371 items from a wide range of UK and US sources. Invaluable reference for anyone with a special interest in this field.

486   HAYES P (1993) 'Transracial adoption: politics and ideology' *Child Welfare* 72, 3, 301-310
Author challenges the social and psychiatric assumptions of opponents of transracial adoption as being rooted in ideology.

487   JOHNSON PR, SHIREMAN JF & WATSON KW (1987) 'Transracial adoption and the development of black identity at age eight' *Child Welfare* 66, 1, 45-55
Paper presents alternative conclusions for and against transracial adoption derived from the same data, demonstrating that 'facts' never speak for themselves.

488   McROY RG & ZURCHER LA (1983) *Transracial and inracial adoptees: the adolescent years* Springfield, Illinois: Charles C Thomas 168pp ISBN 0 398 04840 1
Study of the experiences of black adolescents adopted very young transracially or inracially.

489   RICHARDS B (1987) 'Family, race and identity' *Adoption & Fostering* 11, 3, 10-13
        Article in favour of transracial adoption as an option for black children.

490   SIMON RJ & ALTSTEIN H (1987) *Transracial adoptees and their families: a study of identity and commitment* NY: Praeger 163pp ISBN 0 275 92398 3
        Follow-up study started around 1970 comparing the progress of children living in their own families with others adopted inracially or transracially. The most recent study (children around age 15) found no significant amongst the groups in self-esteem.

491   SMALL J (1991) 'Ethnic and racial identity in adoption within the United Kingdom' *Adoption & Fostering* 15, 4, 61-68
        Discussion of issues around transracial placement in the context of recent research findings.

492   STUBBS P (1987) 'Professionalism and the adoption of black children' *British Journal of Social Work* 17, 473-492
        History and politics of 'same-race' placement debate, with case-studies from two London boroughs.

Birth parents in adoption

Birth parents are the poor relations of the adoption triangle. It is debatable whether 'freeing' children for adoption or dispensing with parental agreement fit at all easily with the Children Act's philosophy of partnership with parents and family support. There is also too much evidence that even those parents who freely consent experience a lack of support at the time and a sense of loss continuing long after the event. Whatever improvements the forthcoming Adoption Act can achieve in this area, there will still be scope for sensitive and empathic work with birth parents before, during and after adoption. The POST-ADOPTION CENTRE 516, 517 and ROLES 518, 519 offer excellent material at the level of practice.

493   BAAF (1992) *If your child is being adopted*

494   BAAF (1992) *Child from the past* (England and Wales)

495   BAAF (1993) *Single, pregnant and thinking about adoption*
        BAAF leaflets for birth parents.

496   BAAF *Step-families and adoption: a guide to the law in Scotland*

BAAF Practice Note 21

497   BELL M (1988) 'The use of freeing orders' *Adoption & Fostering* 12, 2, 10-17
       Article by guardian *ad litem*, using case illustrations.

498   BOUCHIER P, LAMBERT L & TRISELIOTIS J (1991) *Parting with a child for adoption: the mother's perspective* BAAF 136pp ISBN 0 903534
       Study of the characteristics and circumstances of mothers who relinquish their children for adoption.

499   CERVERA NJ (1993) 'Decision making for pregnant adolescents: applying reasoned action theory to research and treatment' *Families in Society* 74, 6, 355-365
       Examines the complex factors in the decision and proposes an empirical model for research and treatment.

500   COCOZZELLI C (1989) 'Predicting the decision of biological mothers to retain or relinquish their babies for adoption: implications for open placement' *Child Welfare* 68, 1, 33-34
       Honolulu study showing three important factors in the decision to relinquish a baby for adoption: life plans that would be disrupted by keeping the baby; more pre-confinement discussions with a social worker; and not wanting to see baby after delivery. The more deprived the mother's background, the more likely she was to choose to keep her baby.

501   DEYKIN EY, PATTI P & RYAN J (1988) 'Fathers of adopted children: a study of the impact of child surrender on birthfathers' *American Journal of Orthopsychiatry* 58, 2, 240-248
       US study indicating that birth fathers also experience a sense of loss when their children are adopted.

502   DOMINICK C (1988) *Early contact in adoption: contact between birthmother and adoptive parents at the time of and after adoption*
       Department of Social Welfare, Wellington, NZ 200pp ISBN 0 477 07257 7
       Report of research study.

503   FIELD J (1990) 'Long-term outcomes for birth mothers before and after reunion' *Adoption & Fostering* 14,3, 14-17

504   FISH A & SPEIRS C (1990) 'Biological parents choose adoptive parents: the use of profiles in adoption' *Child Welfare* 69, 2, 129-139
       Evaluation of a pilot programme in which birth parents chose adopters from a list of profiles provided by the agency, with consumer feedback from the

various parties and discussion of pros and cons in this approach to more open adoption.

505   FITSELL A (1989) 'Relinquishing mothers share experiences' *Adoption & Fostering* 13, 4, 39-41

506   HALL G (1991) 'Adoption and contact with birth families' *Adoption & Fostering* 15, 3, 40-42
Account of work by *Parents for Children* with birth parents who are in contact (or seeking contact) with their children.

507   HILL M, LAMBERT L, TRISELIOTIS J & BUIST M (1992) 'Making judgments about parenting: the example of freeing for adoption' *British Journal of Social Work* 22,4, 373-389
Article derived from 510, seeking to identify key dimensions of parent–child relations which influence social work and court decisions.

508   HOWE D, SAWBRIDGE P & HININGS D (1992) *Half a million women: mothers who lose their children by adoption* Penguin 162pp ISBN 0140154159
Account written in popular style of the pain and grief experienced by birth mothers, advocating a more open approach.

509   LINDSAY JW (1988) *Pregnant too soon: adoption is an option* 219pp 2nd edition California: Morning Glory Press 219pp ISBN 0 930934 25 3
Teenagers' accounts of unmarried parenthood.

510   LAMBERT L, BUIST M, TRISELIOTIS J & HILL M (1990) *Freeing children for adoption* BAAF 158pp ISBN 0 903534 93 2
Research study of 39 children subject of freeing orders in Scotland. Value somewhat limited by restrictions on access to birth parents.

511   LOWE N with BORKOWSKI M, COPNER R, GRIEW K & MURCH M (1993) *Report of the research into the use and practice of the freeing for adoption provisions* Department of Health/HMSO 94pp ISBN 0 11 321589 4
Study by the Socio-Legal Centre for Family Studies at Bristol University.

512   McLAUGHLIN SD, PEARCE SE, MANNINEN DL & WINGES LD (1988) 'To parent or relinquish: consequences for adolescent mothers' *Social Work* 33, 4, 320-324
Comparison of two groups of teenage mothers showed that those who followed through with adoption were more likely to complete vocational training, delay marriage, avoid a rapid further pregnancy, be employed after birth, and to live in higher income households. Less predictably, there

were few differences on measures of self-esteem, and satisfaction with life or with the decision made.

513   MOORE N (1986) *Secret child* Pickering Paperbacks 159pp ISBN 0 7208 0681 X.
Story of the reunion of a mother with her son whom she gave up for adoption 27 years earlier.

514   ODAMS M (1991) 'A decision reversed – mothers who withdraw from having their babies adopted' *Adoption & Fostering* 15, 2, 45-47
Article derived from a small research study.

515   PHILLIPS R (1992) 'The role of social work departments in step-parent adoptions' *Adoption & Fostering* 16, 2, 16-21
Scottish study into the perceptions of social workers and stepfamilies involved in adoption.

516   *POST-ADOPTION CENTRE (1990) *Groups for women who have parted with a child for adoption: reasons for holding birth mothers' groups* London: Post-Adoption Centre 12pp ISBN X 75 168186 4

517   *POST-ADOPTION CENTRE (1990) *Working with mothers who lost a child through adoption* London: Post-Adoption Centre 10pp ISBN X 75 168190 2

518   *ROLES P (1989) *Saying goodbye to a baby vol 1 – the birthparent's guide to loss and grief in adoption* Washington DC: Child Welfare League of America 92pp ISBN 0 87868 387 9

519   *ROLES P (1990) *Saying goodbye to a baby vol 2 – a counsellor's guide to birthparent loss and grief in adoption* Washington DC: Child Welfare League of America 34 pp ISBN 0 87868 393 3

520   SACHDEV P (1991) 'The birth father: a neglected element in the adoption equation' *Families in Society* 72, 3, 131-139
Findings from a study involving adoptive parents, adopted people and adoption workers indicating more sympathy for granting access rights to birth mothers than to fathers. Adopted people largely 'amnesic' about birth fathers' existence, more sympathetic towards birth mothers.

521   SHAWYER J (1979) *Death by adoption* New Zealand: Cicada Press 291pp ISBN 0 908599 02 1
An angry book, born of the author's experience as a single mother and the experiences of other women similarly placed. Includes interviews with birth parents, adopted people, and a social worker equally disenchanted with the system.

522   SCOURFIELD F, HENDRY A et al (1991) 'Unfinished business – the
       experience of a birth mothers' group' *Adoption & Fostering* 15, 2, 36-40
       Descriptive account of a series of group meetings, including contributions
       from mothers themselves.

523   WELLS S (1993) 'Post-traumatic stress disorder in birth mothers' *Adoption
       & Fostering* 17, 2, 30-32

Adoptive parents

Although in practice a good deal of adoption work involves couples (or
single parents) who already have children of their own, there is still a
good deal of literature around the themes of infertility and childlessness
as factors in adoptive parenthood, eg 529, 533, 541, 558. The earlier study
by HUMPHREY 544 also offers vivid insights into the experience of
childlessness. Assessment v preparation also continues to be a live issue
(531, 553, 557), with HARTMAN 539 offering a useful amalgam of the
two processes. KIRK 547 remains unsurpassed for its theoretical and
human understanding of the dilemmas of adoptive parenthood.

524   **AUSTIN J (ed) (1985) *Adoption: the inside story* Barn Owl Books 180pp
       Short articles on 'the problems, pains and pleasures' of adoptive family
       life by members of Parent to Parent Information on Adoption Services.
       The general tone is positive but there is no attempt to gloss over the pain
       and hard work involved.

525   BAAF (1993) *Talking about origins*

526   BAAF (1993) *Children and smoking*
       BAAF Practice Note 30 stressing the need to balance the positive qualities
       of prospective carers who smoke against the adverse effects of smoking
       upon children.

527   BERRY M (1993) 'Adoptive parents' perceptions of, and comfort with,
       open adoption' *Child Welfare* 72, 2 231-253
       Large-scale study of California adopters found them reasonably happy with
       open adoption.

528   BRADBURY SA & MARSH MR (1988) 'Linking families in preadoption
       counseling: a family systems model' *Child Welfare* 67, 4, 327-335.
       Account of how family systems thinking has influenced the policies and
       practice of one agency placing infants for adoption. Pre-placement work
       now involves extended family members from both birth and adoptive parent

families, linking the families to the eventual benefit of all members of the adoption triad.

529   BREBNER CM, SHARP JD & STONE FH (1985) *The role of infertility in adoption* BAAF 75pp ISBN 0 903534 62 2
Material from a longitudinal study of infertile couples adopting, highlighting the impact of their infertility on the process.

530   BROWN, HC (1992) 'Gender, sex and sexuality in the assessment of prospective carers' *Adoption & Fostering* 16, 2, 30-34

531   CAIN P (1992) 'Objectivity and assessment' *Adoption & Fostering* 16, 2, 40-41
Response to RYBURN 553.

532   COHEN JS & WESTHUES A (1990) *Well-functioning families for adoptive and foster children* University of Toronto Press 162pp ISBN 08020 6754 0
Canadian demonstration study of a systems-based training programme for adoption and foster care workers, designed to improve family assessment, matching and the support of the child after placement.

533   DALY K (1990) 'Infertility and adoption readiness' *Families in Society* 71, 8, 483-492
Research study which challenges conventional wisdom that couples need to 'resolve' their feelings on infertility before being ready to enter adoption.

534   **CHENNELLS P (1987) *Explaining adoption to your adopted child: a guide for adoptive parents* BAAF 32pp ISBN 0 903534 71 1

535   DIGIULIO JF (1987) 'Assuming the adoptive parent role' *Social Casework* 68, 9, 561-566
Article reporting a US survey which supports KIRK's thesis (see 547) that adoptions fare better when there is acknowledgment of the differences between biological and adoptive parenthood than where there is denial.

536   FEIGELMAN W & SILVERMAN AR (1983) *Chosen children: new patterns of adoptive relationships* NY: Praeger 261pp ISBN 0 03 062343 X
Study of 'preferential' adopters (adopting for social/humanitarian reasons rather than because of infertility) shows them to be more willing than traditional adopters to consider 'hard-to-place' children, more successful when they do; and more open in communication about adoption with their children.

537   FRATTER J (1989) 'How adoptive parents feel about contact with birth

parents after adoption' *Adoption & Fostering* 13, 4, 18-26
Consumer study.

538   GROZE V (1991) 'Adoption and single parents: a review' *Child Welfare* 70, 3, 321-32
       Review of twelve research studies 1970-1988 comes out strongly in favour of single-parent adoption as being as nurturing and viable as two-parent adoptions.

539   *HARTMAN A (1979) *Finding families: an ecological approach to family assessment in adoption* California: Sage Foundation 107pp ISBN 0 8357 8427 4
       Exposition of the 'ecological' approach, which seeks to involve applicants as partners in the process and to take account of their wider social environment. Guidance on the use of the ecomap, geneogram, and sculpting techniques.

540   *HARTMAN A (1984) *Work with adoptive families beyond placement* NY: Child Welfare League of America 61pp ISBN 0 87868 219 8
       Sequel to 539, applying ecological principles to post-placement and post-adoption work.

541   HOUGHTON D & HOUGHTON P (1984) *Coping with childlessness* Allen & Unwin 176pp ISBN 004131025 X
       Drawing on evidence from the National Association for the Childless the authors demonstrate the sense of stigma still experienced by people who are involuntarily childless. They argue for better facilities for the treatment of infertility as well as for greater understanding.

542   HOWE D & FRASER J (1988) 'Approval vs preparation: adoptive parents' views of the adoption process' *Adoption & Fostering* 12, 4, 29-34
       Study indicating favourable responses to the provision of parentcraft classes for intending adopters.

543   HOWE D (1992) 'Assessing adoptions in difficulty' *British Journal of Social Work* 22, 1, 1-15
       Study of the assessments made by Parents for Children workers of adoptive families experiencing behavioural and relationship difficulties.

544   **HUMPHREY M (1969) *The hostage seekers: a study of childless and adopting couples* Longmans 162pp
       Classic study, still well worth reading for its vivid accounts of the social and personal implications of childlessness.

545   **JONES M (1987) *Everything you need to know about adoption* Sheldon

Press 98pp
Clear straightforward information for prospective adopters on the issues
and practicalities of adoption. An excellent introduction.

546   KANIUK J (1992) 'The use of relationship in the preparation and support
of adopters' *Adoption & Fostering* 16, 2, 47-52
Article stressing the importance of empowering applicants during the
preparation period so as to enable them to take on the complex tasks of
adoptive parenthood.

547   **KIRK HD (1984) *Shared fate: a theory and method of adoptive relations*
Washington: Ben-Simon Publications 202pp ISBN 0 919539 00 0
Classic demonstration of the idea that there is nothing so practical as a
good theory, providing keen insights into the dilemmas of adoptive
parenthood, and stressing the importance of acknowledging rather than
rejecting the differences from 'natural' parenthhood.

548   LEAROYD C (1989) *Matthew: my son's struggle* Queen Anne Press 127pp
ISBN 0 356 14518 2
Personal account of the adoption of a boy born severely disfigured.

549   MUNROE C (1993) *The child within* Children's Society 115pp
ISBN 0 907324 73 8.
Written by his adoptive mother, this book tells the story of a young boy
who had experienced multiple abuse, and traces the first 15 months of his
placement.

550   PENNIE P (1993) 'Adoption panels – room for improvement' *Adoption
& Fostering* 17, 2, 44-47
Article derived from author's experience on two panels.

551   POST-ADOPTION CENTRE (1990) *Preparing people to adopt babies
and young children: the changing pattern of adoption* Post-Adoption
Centre 10pp ISBN X 75 168185 6

552   **ROWE J (1982) *Yours by choice: a guide for adoptive parents* Routledge
& Kegan Paul 188pp ISBN 0 415 04573 8
Everything you would like to have asked while they were assessing you...!
Intended for prospective adopters but useful for anyone interested in
adoption.

553   RYBURN M (1991) 'The myth of assessment' *Adoption & Fostering* 15,
1, 20-27
Author critical of the traditional view that there is an 'objective reality'

which may be uncovered in the assessment process, and argues for a more open, self-assessment approach. For response by CAIN see 531.

554   RYBURN M (1992) 'Advertising for permanent placements' *Adoption & Fostering* 16, 2, 8-16
Study of advertisements for permanent families shows a mismatch between the importance officially accorded to knowledge about origins and the actual content of advertisements.

555   SELWYN J (1991) 'Applying to adopt: the experience of rejection' *Adoption & Fostering* 15, 3, 26-29
Uses case-studies to examine the perceptions and experiences of couples turned down by an adoption agency.

556   SMITH DW & SHERWIN LN (1988) *Mothers and their adopted children – the bonding process* 2nd edition NY: Tiresias Press 208pp
ISBN 0 913292 40 0
Discussion of practice issues derived from US research study.

557   STEVENSON P (1991) 'A model of self-assessment for prospective adopters' *Adoption & Fostering* 15, 3, 30-34
Account of a Children's Society project employing greater openness in the assessment of prospective adopters.

558   *VALENTINE D (ed) (1989) *Infertility and adoption: a guide for social work practice* Haworth Press 189pp ISBN 0 86656 721 6
Collection of papers on a variety of issues in contemporary adoption, including fertility and parenthood, open adoption and placement disruption.

559   VIGUERS ST (1989) *With child: one couple's journey to their adopted children* Southern Illinois University Press 231pp ISBN 0 8093 1498 3
Personal account of experiences from dealing with infertility to the achievement of an adoption order.

Adopted children

As with foster children, the focus in adoption is increasingly on children seen as having special needs, with less concern than in the past as to whether adopted children generally are any more 'problematic' than children brought up in other ways. There is a welcome concern for the meaning of adoption for children themselves (564, 566, 567, 569, 571) and ways of working with children being placed for adoption (561, 570).

560   BOHMAN M (1970) *Adopted children and their families: a follow-up study*

of adopted children, their background, environment and adjustment
Stockholm: Proprius 239pp
Swedish study suggesting that children's adjustment in adoption is
relatively independent of such background variables as circumstances of
pregnancy or birth, social class, age at placement etc. Over-representation
of behaviour disturbances in adopted boys may be related more to the
adoptive situation and the attitudes of the adoptive parents to their former
childlessness.

561   **CIPOLLA J, McGOWN B & YANULIS MA (1992) *Communicating
through play: techniques for assessing and preparing children for adoption*
BAAF 44pp ISBN 1 873868 07 3
UK edition derived from work first published in the USA by Spaulding for
Children, it offers an imaginative range of verbal and non-verbal techniques
of communication.

562   CLARK A (1990) 'The inter-agency placement of a pre-verbal child with
adoptive parents' *Adoption & Fostering* 14, 2, 15-20

563   COHEN NJ, COYNE J & DUVALL J (1993) 'Adopted and biological
children in the clinic: family, parental and child characteristics' *Journal
of Child Psychology and Psychiatry and Allied Disciplines* 34, 4, 545-562
Clinical research study suggesting that, whilst adoptive families have
greater social and psychological resources, the children are at more risk
of removal as the 'solution' to family problems.

564   HARPER J (1993) 'What does she look like? What children want to know
about their birth parents' *Adoption & Fostering* 17, 2, 27-29
Account of a small research study.

565   HOWE D & HININGS D (1987) 'Adopted children referred to a child and
family centre' *Adoption & Fostering* 11, 3, 44-47
Study showing that adopted children are slightly more susceptible to
referral, but cautioning against too-obvious conclusions.

566   HUNTER M (1993) 'Working with the past' *Adoption & Fostering* 17, 1,
31-36
Article by a psychotherapist on issues around sharing information with
adopters and their children.

567   KREMENTZ J (1982) *How it feels to be adopted* Gollancz 108pp. ISBN
0 394 75853 6
Accounts by 19 American children aged 8-16 years.

568   McROY RG, GROTEVANT HD & ZURCHER LA (1988) *Emotional*

disturbance in adopted adolescents: origins and development NY: Praeger
232pp ISBN 0 275 92913 2
Research in which the authors used a variety of theoretical frameworks
with which to investigate emotional disturbance in 100 adopted children
currently in residential treatment centres.

569   MELINA LR (1989) *Making sense of adoption: a parent's guide* NY:
Harper & Row 256pp ISBN 0 06 096319 0

570   PARDEK JT & PARDEK JA (1989) 'Helping children adjust to adoption
through the bibliotherapeutic approach' *Early Child Development and
Care* 44, 31-37
Article outlining the use of bibliotherapy, listing suggested books and
activities.

571   POST-ADOPTION CENTRE (1990) *Explaining adoption to children who
have been adopted: how do we find the right words: the child's
understanding* London: Post-Adoption Centre 15pp ISBN X 75 168187 2

572   SEGLOW J, PRINGLE MK & WEDGE P (1972) *Growing up adopted: a
long-term national study of adopted children and their families* National
Foundation for Educational Research 200pp ISBN 901225 85 1
First major report on the National Child Development Study in relation to
adopted children, indicating that they were doing every bit as well as
children in other kinds of family setting.

573   TRISELIOTIS JP & RUSSELL J (1984) *Hard to place: the outcome of
adoption and residential care* Heinemann 228pp ISBN 0 435 82892 4
Scottish comparative study. A much higher proportion of the adopted group
rated their experiences of growing up positively than did the residential
group. Residential staff seemed to have as much difficulty as adoptive
parents in discussing children's origins.

574   VEEVERS HM (1991) 'Which child, which family?' *Adoption & Fostering*
15, 1, 42-46
Offers a framework for matching in placement derived from transactional
analysis.

Children with special needs

575   BAAF (1989) *Working together in inter-agency placements* BAAF
Loose-leaf binder offering stage-by-stage guidelines on policy and practice
issues.

576   COHEN JS & WESTHUES A (1990) *Well-functioning families for*

adoptive and foster children: a handbook for child welfare workers
University of Toronto Press 176pp ISBN 0 8020 6754 9

577   GROZE VK & ROSENTHAL JA (1991) 'Single parents and their adopted
children' *Families in Society* 72, 2, 67-77
Study of adoptions by couples and single parents of children with special
needs. Marital status had little if any effect on the risk of disruption.

578   GROZE V & ROSENTHAL JA (1991) 'A structural analysis of families
adopting special-needs children' *Families in Society* 72, 8, 469-481
Study showed such families to be particularly adaptable and cohesive, and
characterised by close emotional bonding.

579   HILL M, HUTTON S & EASTON S (1988) 'Adoptive parenting – plus
and minus' *Adoption & Fostering* 12, 2, 17-23
Lothian study of the impact of 'special needs' placements on adopters and
permanent foster carers.

580   HILL M, LAMBERT L & TRISELIOTIS J (1989) *Achieving adoption
with love and money* National Children's Bureau 285pp ISBN 0 902817
41 8
Account of two research studies into the use of adoption allowances.

581   NELSON KA (1985) *On the frontier of adoption: a study of special needs
adoptive families* NY: Child Welfare League of America 110pp ISBN 0
87868 225 2
US study of adopted children over the age of eight who have siblings and
are moderately or severely impaired. High proportion of placements appear
successful, though problems are not minimised – including the feeling of
some families that they were misled into taking a very difficult child.

582   *THOBURN J (1990) *Success and failure in permanent family placement*
Ashgate Publishing Company 105pp ISBN 0 566 07080 4
Reviews literature on special needs adoption and presents a follow-up study
over a five-year period of 21 children adopted from care. Author concludes
that special needs placement is likely to defy attempts at prediction, and
that guidelines can be helpful but cannot replace the painstaking and
intuitive assessment of each case.

583   WESTHUES A & COHEN JS (1990) 'Preventing disruption of
special-needs adoptions' *Child Welfare* 69, 2, 141-155
Preliminary study investigating differences between successful and
unsuccessful special needs adoptions indicates fathers' pivotal role in
maintaining placements – including active involvement in parenting as
well as support for mother.

Older children

584   ASTON E (1981) *Getting to know you* BAAF 44pp ISBN 0 903534 36 3
Booklet designed to promote discussion of the difficulties which parents
and older children (adopted or fostered) face in getting to know one another.

585   BAAF (1987) *Meeting children's needs through adoption and fostering*
Pamphlet addressed to people thinking of adopting or fostering children
with special needs.

586   *BARTH RP & BERRY M (1988) *Adoption and disruption: rates, risks
and responses* NY: Aldine de Gruyter 264pp ISBN 0 202 36054 7
US study of older child adoptions showing a decrease in disruption rate,
largely attributable to greater use of foster parent adoptions. Neither
placements in which siblings were together nor transracial adoptions were
any more likely to disrupt than others. Older children and children with
previous adoptive placements were generally at greatest risk. Classification
of cases using five variables routinely available at placement were highly
predictive of adoption disruptions.

587   BERRY M & BARTH RP (1990) 'A study of disrupted adoptive
placements of adolescents' *Child Welfare* 69, 3, 209-225
Article derived from 586 suggests greater levels of success for foster parent
adoptions, adopters in their forties or older, presence of other foster children
in the home, and an adequate level of adoption subsidy.

588   BERRY M (1990) 'Stress and coping among older child adoptive families'
Social Work and Social Sciences Review 1,2, 71-93
Article emphasising the importance of family, friends and professionals in
the development of families' coping strategies.

589   **DONLEY K (1981) *Opening new doors: finding families for older and
disabled children* BAAF 56pp ISBN 0 903534 33 9
Edited version of talks given by Kay Donley, including her celebrated Ten
Commandments for working with children.

590   FESTINGER T (1986) *Necessary risk: a study of adoptions and disrupted
adoptive placements* NY: Child Welfare League of America 48pp
ISBN 0 87868 245 7
US study of 897 children over the age of six when 12 months into
placement. Long-term disruption rate estimated to be around 13%. Risk
factors included sharing the home with adoptive own children of the
opposite sex, and being placed separately from siblings. Older children
also at more risk of disruption.

591 FRATTER J, NEWTON D & SHINGOLD D (1982) *Cambridge Cottage Pre-Fostering and Adoption Unit* Barnardo Social Work Paper 16 83pp
Account of the work of the unit in preparing children for family placement.

592 **JEWETT CL (1978) *Adopting the older child* Mass: Harvard Common Press 308p ISBN 0 916782 08 5
Offers a wealth of material and ideas on adopting older children, with plentiful use of case examples.

593 KADUSHIN A (1970) *Adopting older children* NY: Columbia University Press 245pp ISBN 0 231 03322 2
One of the earliest studies to encourage the adoption of older children. Based on interviews with 91 sets of adoptive parents whose children were aged 5 or over at placement, it reported a high level of parental satisfaction.

594 KAGAN RM & REID WJ (1986) 'Critical factors in the adoption of emotionally disturbed youths' *Child Welfare* 65, 1, 63-73
US study suggesting as a positive factor the confidence of adoptive parents that they would not follow through on their destructive impulses towards the children. Humour and creative discipline on the part of adoptive fathers was also important See also REID et al 597.

595 KATZ L (1986) 'Parental stress and factors for success in older child adoption' *Child Welfare* 65, 6, 569-578
Author suggests as success factors adopters' tolerance of their own ambivalent feelings, refusal to be rejected by the child; ability to delay own gratification and to value gradual improvement; role flexibility; a firm sense of entitlement, 'intrusive' and controlling qualities exercised in a caring way; humour and self-care; and an open rather than closed family system.

596 KERRANE A, HUNTER A & LANE M (1980) *Adopting older and handicapped children: a consumers' view of the preparation, assessment, placement and post-placement support services* Barnardo Social Work Paper 14 139pp ISBN X 60 204269 X
Consumer study of the New Families Project, Glasgow.

597 REID WJ, KAGAN RM, KAMINSKY A & HELMER K (1987) 'Adoptions of older institutionalized youth' *Social Casework* 68, 3, 140-149
Sequel to 594 urging caution on the adoptive placement of older children with multiple problems, and suggesting that 'professional' parenting may be a more appropriate route to permanence.

598 *RUSHTON A, TRESEDER J & QUINTON D (1986) *New parents for*

older children BAAF 139pp ISBN 0 903534 79 9
Research study into the progress over one year of older children placed for adoption.

599   TIZARD B (1977) *Adoption: a second chance* Open Books 251pp ISBN 0 7291 0196 7
Comparative study suggesting a greater degree of security and 'success' for adopted children as against some other groups, including those returned home.

600   TIZARD B & HODGES J (1990) 'Ex-institutional children: a follow-up study to age 16' *Adoption & Fostering* 14, 1, 17-20

601   TRISELIOTIS J (1985) 'Adoption with contact' *Adoption & Fostering* 9, 4, 19-24
Review in which the author argues for continued contact with the birth family in older child adoptions.

602   WARD M & LEWKO JH (1987) 'Adolescents in families adopting older children: implications for service' *Child Welfare* 66, 6, 539-547
Study unusual in focusing on adolescent own-children of adoptive parents.

Children with medical conditions and disabilities

603   **ARGENT H (1984) *Find me a family: the story of Parents for Children* Souvenir Press 205pp
An account of a pioneer agency in the placement of children with special needs.

604   BROWN E (1988) 'Recruiting adoptive parents for children with developmental disabilities' *Child Welfare* 67, 2, 123-135.

605   GLIDDEN LM (1985) 'Adopting mentally handicapped children: family characteristics' *Adoption & Fostering* 9, 3, 53-56

606   GLIDDEN LM (1990) *Formed families: adoption of children with handicaps* Haworth Press 242pp ISBN 0866569146
Reports on a follow-up study of permanent placements with largely positive outcomes.

607   HOLLAND A & MURRAY R (1985) 'The genetics of schizophrenia and its implications' *Adoption & Fostering* 9, 2, 39-46.

608   KANIUK J & FAIRHURST J (1988) 'The direct placement for adoption of a baby with spina bifida' *Adoption & Fostering* 12, 4, 40-43
Case study and discussion.

609   *MACASKILL C (1985) *Against the odds: adopting mentally handicapped children* BAAF 100pp ISBN 0 903534 58 4
Research study of 20 families.

610   MACASKILL C (1988) '"It's a bonus" – families experiences of adopting children with disabilities' *Adoption & Fostering* 12, 2, 24-28
Article discussing themes emerging from a follow-up of 609.

611   OXTOBY M (ed) (1982) *Genetics in adoption and fostering: guidelines and resources* BAAF 44pp ISBN 0 903534 41 X
Includes a paper on genetics and adoption, and material from a BAAF medical group working party on genetic conditions and their implications for social workers in adoption, fostering and child care generally.

612   ROSENTHAL JA, GROZE V & AGUILAR GD (1991) 'Adoption outcomes for children with handicaps' *Child Welfare* 70, 6, 623-636
Questionnaire study of 800 families reports favourably – the presence of a handicap was not an important factor in influencing outcome.

613   *SAWBRIDGE P (ed) (1983) *Parents for children: twelve practice papers* BAAF 88pp ISBN 0 903534 44 4
Collection of papers dealing with various aspects of placing children with special needs.

614   *WEDGE P & THOBURN J (eds) (1986) *Finding families for 'hard-to-place' children: evidence from research* BAAF 96pp ISBN 0 903534 00 2
Contributions on the work of Parents for Children, post-adoption support, children with medical and developmental problems, and family placement projects in Essex and Norfolk.

615   WOLKIND S (ed) (1979) *Medical aspects of adoption and foster care* Heinemann 102pp ISBN 0433 36905 1
Collection of papers dealing with issues such as handicap, child abuse, incest and AID.

Sibling groups

616   JONES M & NIBLETT R (1985) 'To split or not to split: the placement of siblings' *Adoption & Fostering* 9, 2, 26-29.

617   WARD M (1987) 'Choosing adoptive families for large sibling groups' *Child Welfare* 66, 3, 259-268

618   WEDGE P & MANTLE G (1991) *Sibling groups and social work* Avebury 107pp ISBN 1 85628 195 7

Research study of siblings referred to adoption agencies for permanent placement, focussing on reasons for splitting or not splitting.

Adults adopted as children

619   BEGLEY VJ (1988) *Missing links* Chevy Chase USA: Claycombe Press Inc 224pp ISBN 0 933905 06 8
Personal account of search for origins.

620   COPEMAN T (1989) *Mother's son: the astonishing story of a man's 26 year quest to find his mother* Maclean Dubois 99pp

621   HAIMES E & TIMMS N (1985) *Adoption, identity and social policy: the search for distant relatives* Gower 105pp 0 566 00888 2
Research study dealing with, amongst other matters, issues around 'compulsory counselling' for people seeking access to their adoption records.

622   HANDEL AG (1992) 'Growing up adopted' *Adoption & Fostering* 16, 1, 39-41
Personal account of an adopted person.

623   JAFFEE B & FANSHEL D (1970) *How they fared in adoption: a follow-up study* NY: Columbia University Press 370pp ISBN 0 231 03420 2
Analysis of research interviews with adoptive parents of 100 young adults, with some useful material on 'entitlement'. See also 624

624   JAFFEE B (1974) 'Adoption outcome: a two-generation view' *Child Welfare* 53, 4, 211-224
Interviews with some of the young adults whose adoptive parents' experiences were reported in 623, showing important differences in perception, notably in the area of telling about adoption and having information about origins.

625   LINDSAY M & McGARRY K (1985) *Adoption counselling: a talking point* Dr Barnardo's Scottish Division 79pp
Account of the work of the Scottish Adoption Advisory Service.

626   POST-ADOPTION CENTRE (1990) *Adoption issues for lesbian women* London: Post-Adoption Centre 5pp X 75 168189 9

627   RAYNOR L (1980) *The adopted child comes of age* Allen & Unwin 166pp ISBN 0 04 362030 2
Retrospective study of young adults placed as children by the Thomas Coram Foundation, based on case-records and interviews.

81

628   SACHDEV P (1992) 'Adoption reunion and after: a study of the search process and experience of adoptees' *Child Welfare* 71, 1, 53-68
Canadian research study of 124 adopted adults who sought and achieved a reunion with their birth mothers or other relatives.

629   TRISELIOTIS J (1973) *In search of origins: the experiences of adopted people* Routledge & Kegan Paul 177pp ISBN 0 71000 7534 0
Scottish study (making vivid use of interview material) which helped the move to extend to English and Welsh adopted adults the right to obtain their original birth certificates.

630   TUGENDHAT J (1992) *The adoption triangle: searching and uniting* Bloomsbury Publ Ltd 117pp ISBN 0 7475 1010 5
Popular style account by family therapist of adopted adults' efforts to find birth parents and families.

631   WHEELER J (1990) 'The secret is out' *Adoption & Fostering* 14, 3, 22-28
Personal account of a search for knowledge about the writer's origins, with some information about US self-help organisations in this field.

Post-adoption services

632   ARGENT H (ed) (1984) *Keeping the doors open: a review of post-adoption services* BAAF 126pp ISBN 0 903534 75 4
Papers on consumer and agency viewpoints with contributions on black children in black families, specialist ventures, adoption and therapy, and the position in the US.

633   BAAF *The Adoption Contact Register (England and Wales)* BAAF Practice Note 20

634   ELBOW M & KNIGHT M (1987) 'Adoption disruption: losses, transitions and tasks' *Social Casework* 68, 9, 546-552
Authors argue that endings need proper handling, including use of a disruption conference and disruption story for the child.

635   FEAST J (1992) 'Working in the adoption circle: outcomes of s.51 counselling' *Adoption & Fostering* 16, 4, 46-52
Research on the dilemmas for adopted adults and their counsellors.

636   FEAST J & SMITH J (1993) 'Working on behalf of birth families – the Children's Society experience' *Adoption & Fostering* 17, 2, 33-40
Early findings from the Post-Adoption Project, acting as intermediary between birth parents and adopted people.

637   HODGKINS P (1991) *Birth records counselling: a practical guide* BAAF

72pp ISBN 0 903534 97 5
Practical manual for workers providing birth records counselling to adopted
people, with checklists, details of helpful organisations and information
on the legal position in the UK.

638 HOGGAN P (1991) 'Attitudes to post-placement support services in
permanent family placement' *Adoption & Fostering* 15, 1, 28-30
Article based on Lothian experience.

639 HOWE D (1987) 'Adopted children in care' *British Journal of Social
Work* 17, 493-505
Report of a research study in three social services departments, 1985-86.

640 HOWE D (1990) 'The Post-Adoption Centre: the first three years' *Adoption
& Fostering* 14, 1, 27-31

641 HOWE D (1990) 'The consumers' view of the Post-adoption Centre'
Adoption & Fostering 14, 2, 32-36
Report of a consumer study.

642 LAMBERT L, BORLAND M, HILL M & TRISELIOTIS J (1992) 'Using
contact registers in adoption searches' *Adoption & Fostering* 16, 1, 42-45

643 NATIONAL ORGANISATION FOR THE COUNSELLING OF
ADOPTEES AND PARENTS (1988) *Searching for family connections*
NORCAP 24pp ISBN 0 9509901 0 8
Guide to seeking out birth records, written primarily for adopted people.

644 PHILLIPS R (1988) 'Post-adoption services – the views of adopters'
Adoption & Fostering 12, 4, 24-29
Account of a Scottish research study.

645 SAWBRIDGE P (1988) 'The Post-Adoption Centre – what are the users
teaching us?' *Adoption & Fostering* 12,1, 5-12

646 SAWBRIDGE P (1990) 'Post-adoption counselling: what do we actually
do?' *Adoption & Fostering* 14, 1, 31-35

647 SLAYTOR P (1988) 'Reunion and resolution: the adoption triangle'
Adoption & Fostering 12, 2, 31-37

648 STAFFORD G (1993) *Where to find adoption records: a guide for
counsellors* BAAF 124pp ISBN 1 873868 09 X
Revised and updated version of an invaluable reference book for adoption
counsellors.

649   TRISELIOTIS J (1988) 'Adoption services and counselling' *Adoption &
       Fostering* 12, 2, 31-37

Intercountry adoption

Intercountry adoption is transracial placement writ large and raises the
same debates and emotions. Even writers broadly sympathetic to the idea
of intercountry adoption tend to be cautious in their advocacy and keen
to press for strict safeguards.

650   ALTSTEIN H & SIMON RJ (eds)(1990) *Intercountry adoption – a
       multinational perspective* Praeger 204pp ISBN 0 275 93287 7
       Account of the development of intercountry adoption and the experiences
       of families and children adopted in this way in the USA, Western Europe
       and Israel.

651   BAAF (1991) *Inter-country adoption: a survey of agencies* BAAF 36pp
       ISBN 1 873868 00 6
       Survey of agency practice in English, Welsh and Scottish agencies.

652   BAAF *Inter-country adoption (Scotland)* BAAF Practice Note 24

653   *BAGLEY C, YOUNG L & SCULLY A (1993) *International and
       transracial adoptions: a mental health perspective* Avebury Publ 366pp
       ISBN 1 85628 082 9
       Examines several studies focusing on the adjustment and mental health of
       children placed via intercountry or transracial adoption.

654   DUNCAN W (1993) 'The Hague Convention on the protection of children
       and co-operation in respect of intercountry adoption' *Adoption & Fostering*
       17, 3 9-13
       Article outlining the key provisions of the Convention and noting issues
       arising for the UK.

655   HOCKSBERGEN RAC (ed) (1986) *Adoption in worldwide perspective: a
       review of programs, policies and legislation in 14 countries* Lisse: Swets
       & Zeitlinger 242pp Available from Adoption Centre, University of Utrecht,
       Heidelberglaan 1, Utrecht-Vithof, Holland ISBN 90 265 0738 0
       Short papers from adoption experts each reviewing the adoption scene in
       their own country. Much on intercountry adoption, surprisingly little on
       children with special needs.

656   HUMPHREY M & HUMPHREY J (1992) *Inter-country adoption:
       practical experiences* Routledge 192pp ISBN 0 415 05210 6

Case studies of eight families who undertook intercountry adoption in the 1980s.

657   NGABONZIZA D (1991) 'Moral and political issues facing relinquishing countries' *Adoption & Fostering* 15, 4, 75-80
Article strongly critical of intercountry adoption as an attempt at individualised solutions to a global problem – most children involved are victims of poverty rather than abandonment.

658   REICH D (1990) 'Children of the nightmare' *Adoption & Fostering* 14, 3, 9-14
Examines the issue of intercountry adoption against the background of the plight of Romanian children after the 1990 revolution.

659   SELMAN P (1993) 'Services for intercountry adoption in the UK: some lessons from Europe' *Adoption & Fostering* 17, 3, 14-19.
UK policy issues examined in the light of developments in the Netherlands and Sweden.

660   TIZARD B (1991) 'Intercountry adoption: a review of the evidence' *Journal of Child Psychology and Psychiatry* 32, 5, 743-756
Outcome studies tend to show positive results but author questions the lack of attention to identity and racism.

661   TRISELIOTIS J (1991) 'Inter-country adoption' *Adoption & Fostering* 15, 4, 46-52
Overview of research findings and discussion of current controversies.

Books for children about adoption and fostering

There is now a wealth of colourful and attractive material aimed at young children facing family crises of various kinds and it is impossible in the space available to do more than draw attention to some examples. BAAF, the Children's Society and NFCA not only produce material of their own but regularly issue booklists which generously publicise 'rival' publications. The titles listed below are nicely produced with illustrations, usually in colour. The US material is often imaginative and innovative (for example, in its inclusion of minority ethnic children and families) but the sugar-content is often rather high for British tastes.

A notable feature of most such publications is the lack of attention to issues of contact with natural parents or the possibility of eventual return to the family. It really is time someone introduced writers of children's books to the Children Act – an updated edition would surely find a ready market amongst social workers and carers.

662   ALTHEA (1980) *Jane is adopted* Souvenir Press Ltd 23pp ISBN 285 62457 1
       Story explaining adoption for younger children.

663   ALTHEA (1984) *My new family* Cambridge: Dinosaur Publ Ltd 32pp ISBN 0 85122 393 1
       Story of young girl moving from residential to foster family care.

664   ALTON H (1987) *Moving pictures* BAAF ISBN 0 903534 73 8
       Workbook for use with children facing a move.

665   ANDERSON D & FINNE M (1986) *Jason's story: going to a foster home* Macmillan 48pp ISBN 0 87518 324 7

666   ANGEL A (1988) *Real for sure sister* Indianapolis: Perspectives Press 69pp ISBN 0 9609504 7 8
       Story of four children placed by intercountry adoption.

667   ARMSTRONG L (1989) *Solomon says: a speakout on foster care* NY: Simon & Schuster 272pp ISBN 0 65782 8

668   BAAF (1988) *My health passport* BAAF 12pp
       Record booklet particularly suitable for children being looked after by local authorities.

669   BRODZINSKY AB (1986) *The mulberry bird: story of an adoption* Indianapolis: Perspectives Press 44p ISBN 0 9609504 5 1
       Written for children aged 5-10 years.

670   BYARS B (1977) *The pinballs* Puffin Books 93pp ISBN 0 0403 1121 1
       Story of three foster children, recommended for readers aged 10-12 years.

671   GABEL S (1989) *Where the sun kisses the sea* Indianapolis: Perspectives Press 27pp ISBN 0 944934 00 5
       Story of a child placed via intercountry adoption.

672   KING P (1989) *Talking pictures* BAAF ISBN 0 903534 77 0
       Workbook for social workers to use with children, especially those experiencing separation.

673   KOCH J (1985) *Our baby: a birth and adoption story* Indianapolis: Perspectives Press 28pp ISBN 0 9609504 4 3
       Unusual in that it deals in story form with birth as well as adoption.

674 McLIVER C & THOM M (1990) *Family talk: picture sheets for children whose family is adopting or fostering* BAAF ISBN 0 903534
Illustrated workbook for parents to use with children aged 6-11 years.

675 MOORE C & LANE M (1992) *Meeting your guardian ad litem* Children's Society 24pp ISBN 0 907324 12 6
Colouring book format for children aged 3-8.

676 NATIONAL FOSTER CARE ASSOCIATION (1990) *My book about me* NFCA 12pp ISBN 0 946015 74 0
Life story book for social workers or carers to use with children recently placed with a foster family.

677 NERLOVE E (1985) *Who is David? a story of an adopted adolescent and his friends* NY: Child Welfare League of America 113pp ISBN 0 87868 233 3
Story for older children of teenage boy attending a workshop for young people who have been adopted.

678 NYSTROM C (1987) *Andy's big question: where do I belong? A child's guide to adoption* Herts: Lion Publishing 39pp ISBN 0 9609504 4 3
Intended for older children who have been adopted, this illustrated story deals with questions of identity &c.

679 ORRITT B (1990) *Dennis duckling – going into care* Children's Society 24pp ISBN 0 907324 52 5
For children aged 3-8 years entering care or joining a new family.

680 THOM M & McLIVER C (1986) *Bruce's story* Children's Society 32pp ISBN 0 907324 27 4
Written as an aid for foster carers and social workers or anyone working with young children who have experienced disruption in their lives. With worksheets for children themselves.

681 VAN DER MEER R & A (1980) *Joey* Heinemann 32pp ISBN 434 97102 2
Story of small boy settling into new foster home.

Title index

Some titles have been abbreviated in the Index – see main entry for full titles. In keeping with normal practice, and the style followed in this bibliography, titles of books and other publications, such as leaflets, appear in italics while titles of articles in journals/periodicals appear in roman.

Author index

A

Adamec C   417
Adcock M   015, 122
Aguilar GD   612
Ahmad B   074
Ahmed S   069
Aldgate J   086, 175, 184, 185, 193,
    211, 225, 226, 227, 230, 236, 237,
    238, 272, 347, 348
Allen N   020
Almas T   260
Althea   662, 663
Alton H   664
Altstein H   490, 650
Anderson D   665
Angel A   666
Archard D   087
Argent H   603, 632
Armstrong L   667
Ashcroft C   055
Ashford S   239
Aston E   584
Atkinson C   240
Auestad A   376
Austin J   524

B

BAAF   021, 022, 070, 088, 241, 359,
    388, 418-421, 472, 493-496, 525,
    526, 575, 585, 633, 651, 652, 668
Bagley C   480, 653
Baily P   124
Baines B   051
Bainham A   011

Bane W   281
Banks N   071, 320
Barker M   144, 145
Barn R   072
Barth RP   422, 586, 587
Bassi J   367
Batty D   089, 090, 186, 187, 360,
    361, 377, 444
Bayley N   089
Bean P   423
Bebbington A   132, 284
Begley VJ   619
Bell M   497
Benedict M   188
Benet MK   424
Benjamin M   123
Berridge D   190, 242
Berry M   422, 456, 527, 586-588
Biehal M   393
Biggs V   091, 092
Biggs   V1992
Black D   073
Blanchard A   455
Blanton TL   457
Bloksberg LM   217
Blumenthal K   273
Blunden G   285
Boer F   368
Bohman M   560
Bolden BJ   410
Bonnerjea L   394
Booth C   161
Borkowski M   443, 511
Borland M   332, 642

110